"This generation of Christians inhabit cultures that sometimes reject not only biblical revelation about reality but also the reality of reality itself. The Questions for Restless Minds series poses many of the toughest questions faced by young Christians to some of the world's foremost Christian thinkers and leaders. Along the way, this series seeks to help the Christian next generation to learn how to think biblically when they face questions in years to come that perhaps no one yet sees coming."

—Russell Moore,
public theologian, *Christianity Today*

"If you're hungry to go deeper in your faith, wrestle with hard questions, and are dissatisfied with the shallow content on your social media newsfeed, you'll really appreciate this series of thoughtful deep dives on critically important topics like faith, the Bible, friendship, sexuality, philosophy, and more. As you engage with some world-class Christian scholars, you'll be encouraged, equipped, challenged, and above all invited to love God more with your heart, soul, mind, and strength."

—Andy Kim,
multiethnic resource director, InterVarsity Christian Fellowship

T0334466

What Is Islam?

Questions for Restless Minds

Questions for Restless Minds

QUESTIONS FOR RESTLESS MINDS

What Is Islam?

Chawkat Moucarry

D. A. Carson,
Series Editor

LEXHAM PRESS

What Is Islam?
Questions for Restless Minds, edited by D. A. Carson

Copyright 2021 Christ on Campus Initiative

Lexham Press, 1313 Commercial St., Bellingham, WA 98225
LexhamPress.com

Print ISBN 9781683594994
Digital ISBN 9781683595007
Library of Congress Control Number 2021937714

Lexham Editorial: Todd Hains, Abigail Stocker, Danielle Thevenaz, Mandi Newell,
Cover Design: Brittany Schrock
Interior Design and Typesetting: Abigail Stocker, ProjectLuz.com

The Christ on Campus Initiative exists to inspire students on college and university campuses to think wisely, act with conviction, and become more Christlike by providing relevant and excellent evangelical resources on contemporary issues.

Visit christoncampuscci.org.

Contents

Series Preface

D. A. CARSON, SERIES EDITOR

THE ORIGIN OF this series of books lies with a group of faculty from Trinity Evangelical Divinity School (TEDS), under the leadership of Scott Manetsch. We wanted to address topics faced by today's undergraduates, especially those from Christian homes and churches.

If you are one such student, you already know what we have in mind. You know that most churches, however encouraging they may be, are not equipped to prepare you for what you will face when you enroll at university.

It's not as if you've never known any winsome atheists before going to college; it's not as if you've never thought about Islam, or the credibility of the New Testament documents, or the nature of friendship, or gender identity, or how the claims of Jesus sound too exclusive and rather narrow, or the nature of evil. But up until now you've probably thought about such things within the shielding cocoon of a community of faith.

Now you are at college, and the communities in which you are embedded often find Christian perspectives to be at best oddly quaint and old-fashioned, if not repulsive. To use the current jargon, it's easy to become socialized into a new community, a new world.

How shall you respond? You could, of course, withdraw a little: just buckle down and study computer science or Roman history (or whatever your subject is) and refuse to engage with others. Or you could throw over your Christian heritage as something that belongs to your immature years and buy into the cultural package that surrounds you. Or—and this is what we hope you will do—you could become better informed.

But how shall you go about this? On any disputed topic, you do not have the time, and probably not the interest, to bury yourself in a couple of dozen volumes written by experts for experts. And if you did, that would be on *one* topic—and there are scores of topics that will grab the attention of the inquisitive student. On the other hand, brief pamphlets with predictable answers couched in safe slogans will prove to be neither attractive nor convincing.

So we have adopted a middle course. We have written short books pitched at undergraduates who want arguments that are accessible and stimulating, but invariably courteous. The material is comprehensive enough that it has become an important resource for pastors and other campus leaders who devote their energies to work with students. Each book ends with a brief annotated bibliography and study questions, intended for readers who want to probe a little further.

Lexham Press is making this series available as attractive print books and in digital formats (ebook and Logos resource). We hope and pray you will find them helpful and convincing.

1

INTRODUCTION

I SLAM CLAIMS THAT Judaism, Christianity, and Islam itself are three God-given religions. All prophets (including Moses, Jesus, and Muhammad) preached essentially the same message: God is one, and everyone must obey and worship him because on the day of judgment people will be sent to paradise or to hell according to whether or not they believed in their Creator and complied with his laws. This theological inclusiveness is only apparent since Islam is believed to be the only saving religion (3:19, 85).[1] It comes at an exceedingly high price for the Christian faith. Indeed, Islam denies the reliability of the Christian Scripture, which contradicts the Qur'an on at least three key issues: God's holy Trinity, the uniqueness of Jesus Christ, and God's saving grace supremely demonstrated in the death and resurrection of Christ. The first four sections of this book examine and respond to Islamic criticisms of the Christian faith.

In its own way, Christianity is no less exclusive. As Eckhard Schnabel puts it,

> The message of the early Christian mission is "exclusive" in terms of the offer of the forgiveness of sins, salvation and justification on judgment day by faith in Jesus the crucified and risen Messiah; it is

"inclusive" in terms of people of all nations, tribes and languages being invited and called to believe in Jesus Christ.[2]

The New Testament presents Jesus Christ as God's perfect and final revelation for all nations, which rules out any further divine revelation, including Islam. Nevertheless, as a world religion Islam cannot and should not be dismissed without thoughtful and courteous engagement. We need to explain, for instance, why the Islamic credentials for Muhammad's prophethood are unconvincing (chapter 6) and how Islamic law is so different from the gospel (chapter 7).

At the same time, there is no doubt that as monotheistic religions Christianity and Islam share significant common ground despite their theological disagreements. This common ground needs to be appreciated if our interaction with Islam is to be informed and fair. This book explains why the gospel, unlike the Qur'an, is indeed good news for all who heed it, including Muslims. It is good news because it is about God's universal and undeserved love for people drawn from every language, ethnicity, and nation.

2

THE
CHRISTIAN
SCRIPTURE

JUDAISM, CHRISTIANITY, AND Islam are monotheistic religions. This means that Jews, Christians, and Muslims worship one God, the Creator. They believe that God has revealed his word in the form of books known as the Holy Scriptures: the Bible and the Qur'an.

For Christians the Bible is divided into two main parts: the Old Testament (written before Jesus Christ) and the New Testament (written in the first century after Jesus Christ).[3] According to the Qur'an, God revealed the Torah to Moses, the Zabur (i.e., the Psalms) to David, and the Injil (i.e., the Gospel) to Jesus before he finally conveyed the Qur'an to Muhammad through the angel Gabriel. This is why Jews and Christians are described in the Qur'an as "the People of the Book."[4]

Muslims believe that the Bible has been altered. This is how they account for the discrepancies that exist between the Qur'an and the Bible. These discrepancies do not represent a real problem for Christians since they do not accept the Qur'an as God's revealed word.

FALSIFICATION THEORIES

Taḥrif is the Arabic word for falsification. The verb *ḥarrafa* ("to falsify") occurs four times in the Qur'an (2:75; 4:46; 5:13, 41). The meaning of these texts is unclear. We have no idea as to when the falsification happened (in the time of Moses, Jesus, or Muhammad?), what "Word" was falsified (the Torah, Gospel, or Qur'an itself?), who did it (Jews and Christians, Jews only, or just some of them?), where (in Israel, Arabia, or somewhere else?), and how (orally or textually?). Muslim scholars trying to answer these questions are divided into two main groups, each comprising highly respected theologians.

The first group contends that the *text* of the Bible has been corrupted. Proponents include Ibn Ḥazm (d. 456/1064), Juwayni (d. 478/1085), and Ibn Taymiyya (d. 728/1328).[5] When Nebuchadnezzar destroyed Jerusalem and its temple (in the sixth century BC), they say, the Hebrew Scriptures were also destroyed. It was only after some Jews returned from their exile in Babylon that one of their leaders, Ezra, wrote the Torah. Because Ezra was not a prophet, his writing was defective. As for the New Testament, the distortion of Jesus' teaching in the Gospels is attributed to two "gaps," namely, a language gap (the Gospels were written in Greek whereas Jesus spoke in Aramaic) and a time gap (the Gospels were written several decades after the events had taken place). Those who believe in this alleged textual falsification assert that God revealed one Gospel to Jesus (according to the Qur'an) whereas Christians have four Gospels. None of these Gospels is ascribed to Jesus, and it is claimed that they often contradict each other. As for the other writings of the New Testament, Muslims do not know what to make of them since they were written by followers of Jesus who were not themselves prophets.[6] Today the vast majority of Muslims believe in the textual falsification of the Bible. They are not even aware that an alternative view exists.

The second group contends that the *meaning* of the Bible, not the text itself, has been changed. Proponents include highly respected Muslim scholars such as Baqillani (d. 403/1013), Ghazali (d. 505/1111), Razi (d. 606/1209), and 'Abduh (d. 1323/1905). Razi, in his *Great Commentary*, argues that God's word must reflect God's attributes. Therefore to say that God let his word (i.e., Torah and Gospel) become untruthful is to undermine God's truthfulness and trustworthiness. Muhammad 'Abduh uses a rational argument in his renowned Qur'anic commentary *Tafsir al-Manar*. The fact that the Scriptures were so widely spread made it impossible for Jews and Christians to modify them even if they wanted to. For this group of scholars, falsification can be understood only in terms of wrong interpretation of biblical texts about, for instance, Jesus Christ. Misinterpretations of the Torah and the Gospel can now be dispelled, Razi observes, since we find in the Qur'an the plain meaning of the Bible.

INSPIRATION VERSUS RECITATION

The Islamic charge against the reliability of the Bible raises some important issues. One issue is the difference between the Christian and the Islamic understandings of revelation.

INSPIRATION

Christians believe that God revealed his word by *inspiration*. This means God did not bypass the human writers of the Bible. On the contrary he led them by his Holy Spirit to write down his word, using their individual personalities and taking into account the historic and cultural contexts of the people for whom their writings were first intended (2 Pet 1:20–21).[7] In other words the human authors of the Bible were actively involved in the process of writing down divine revelation. For instance, the gospel proclaimed by Jesus Christ is one message, yet it is written in four versions, namely, the four Gospels. Thus the gospel of Jesus Christ may be read in Matthew's Gospel as well as in that of Mark, Luke, or John. Moreover, Jesus spoke with his disciples in Aramaic, which was the language spoken by Jews living in Palestine at that time. The four Gospels, however, were written in Greek because they were addressed to different ethnic groups who used Greek as their common language.

Consequently, the Bible is at the same time *God's word*, which guarantees its trustworthiness, and *the word of men*, which underlines its humanness. The human authorship of Scripture means that we can study the Bible the way we study other books. We take into account what kind of text it is (historical, poetic, prophetic, narrative, legislative, apocalyptic, wisdom literature, etc.) and thus decide how we should go about interpreting it. The divine authorship of Scripture, on the other hand, means that we must also approach the Bible with due humility as we seek to understand and obey God's word.

RECITATION

By contrast the Prophet Muhammad's role was to learn the Qur'an by heart and to preach it to his fellow citizens in Mecca and Medina. It was communicated to him word for word. He was not to intervene in the shaping of the message but was to recite literally the words he heard. The verb *qara'a* usually means to read, whereas in a religious context, as here, it means to proclaim or to recite the word of God. The word *qur'an* comes from the same root and thus means the ritual recitation of the sacred text. By extension the word has come to refer to the text itself. The fact that the Qur'an was dictated to Muhammad in this way means that the Islamic Scripture is God's word and God's word alone. This is why the Qur'anic text is usually in the first person plural, this being the plural of divine majesty. Thus recitation, *qira'a*, indicates the way Muhammad received and transmitted God's word.

Since Muhammad was an Arab, the Qur'an was revealed to him in Arabic. The difference between *inspiration* and *recitation* explains why for Muslim readers the Bible looks too much like a human book to be God's word. It also accounts for the fact that the Bible remains God's word when translated into other languages whereas the Qur'an is God's word only in Arabic.

GOD HIMSELF VERSUS
GOD'S WILL

The Islamic Scripture does not reveal who God is for fear of undermining his transcendence. The Qur'an discloses only God's will expressed in his law in order to enable human creatures to obey their Creator and worship him. As one Muslim scholar puts it, "You may not have complete transcendence and self-revelation at the same time."[8] This is quite different from the way Christians think about their Scripture. The Bible claims to reveal God's will as well as God himself.

For Christians, God's revelation reached its climax two thousand years ago: Jesus Christ is God's supreme revelation, God's word manifested in the form of a human being (John 1:1, 10, 14). The Scriptures point to Jesus Christ, and Jesus Christ points to God (Rev 1:1–2; 19:10). God is both transcendent (radically different from his creation) and immanent (he revealed himself in a human person).

INTERPRETING THE
SCRIPTURES

The Bible is a collection of sixty-six books written by over thirty authors over at least thirteen centuries. By contrast the Qur'an was given to one man over twenty-three years. Each Scripture has its distinctive characteristics.

As far as possible one must understand each Scripture by itself before comparing it with the other Scripture. Common rules of interpretation apply to both Scriptures (e.g., respecting the historical context, interpreting Scripture by Scripture, taking into account various literary genres). One must attempt to understand the Scriptures without submitting them to a naturalistic form of human rationality. An open-minded, prejudice-free approach dispels many discrepancies between the Bible and the Qur'an. Some discrepancies, however, are irreconcilable.

EVIDENCE FOR THE
RELIABILITY OF THE BIBLE

The charge that the Torah and the Gospel have undergone textual corruption contains serious flaws. Here are some arguments that show that the Bible is trustworthy.

QUR'ANICAL EVIDENCE: THE
QUR'AN COMMENDS THE BIBLE

Several texts in the Qur'an claim that the Qur'an confirms previous Scriptures (2:41, 89, 91, 97, 101; 3:3, 81). Would the Qur'an confirm the Torah and the Gospel if they were corrupted? The Torah is described as "light and guidance for humankind" (6:91), and the Gospel is depicted in similar terms (5:46). Would these Christian Scriptures be portrayed in this way if they were tampered with?

THEOLOGICAL EVIDENCE: GOD'S WORD
MUST REFLECT HIS ATTRIBUTES

Razi argues that textual corruption of the Scriptures is inconsistent with God's truthfulness. If his word was not reliable, he would not be reliable either. This is why the

Qur'an insists, "There is nothing that can alter the Words of God" (6:34; compare 10:64; 18:27).

Similar claims are made by both religions regarding their respective Scriptures. In the Bible, God himself guarantees that he will protect his word from alteration (Ps 119:89). Jesus confirms that God's word is unchangeable: "It is easier for heaven and earth to disappear than for the least stroke of a pen to drop out of the Law" (Luke 16:17). Similarly in the Qur'an, Allah says, "We have sent down the Message and We Ourselves watch over it" (15:9). The way this is worked out in the two religions is sometimes quite different—especially with respect to how the original revelation each claims has been preserved. This is not the place to probe these differences. For our purposes, I shall focus on the Christian heritage.

SCIENTIFIC EVIDENCE: THE MANUSCRIPTS ARE RELIABLE AND PREDATE ISLAM'S BIRTH

Translations of the Bible are based on the same Hebrew and Greek manuscripts. The material evidence for the corruption or authenticity of the Scriptures lies with these manuscripts. Their study has confirmed the integrity of the Bible. Far from being a handicap, the very existence of many manuscripts has enabled scholars to establish that the text of the Bible has been amazingly well transmitted. Regardless of their religious convictions, the manuscript experts agree that the Bible has been handed down with exceptional accuracy.[9]

Some Greek manuscripts of the whole Bible (Old and New Testaments) predate the birth of Islam. The Codex Sinaiticus (preserved in the British Museum in London) and the Codex Vaticanus (kept in the Vatican library) are from the fourth century. The Codex Alexandrinus (also in the British Museum) is from the fifth century. Some partial New Testament manuscripts date from as early as the second century; most of our oldest Old Testament manuscripts date from the first two centuries before Christ. When compared with later manuscripts, these manuscripts exhibit copyists' errors of various kinds, but not one such error affects any fundamental teaching of the Bible, however minor. More importantly for our purpose, these later manuscripts show that the text of the Bible has not been changed one bit as a result of Jews and Christians not accepting Muhammad as God's prophet.

RATIONAL EVIDENCE: FALSIFICATION DOES NOT MAKE SENSE

Muhammad 'Abduh points out that the widespread propagation of the Scriptures made it virtually impossible that anyone could have tampered with them. Any attempt was not only doomed to failure for practical reasons; it was bound to be discovered and disowned. The animosity between Jews and Christians meant that if either community had tried to change the Scriptures, the other would have denounced them.

Not only were the Christian Scriptures widely scattered but they were translated into different languages. By the time of Christ, the Old Testament was available in Greek; by the end of the third century most of the New Testament had been translated into Latin, Syriac, and Coptic. The New Testament was also quoted in Christian writings as early as the second century.

THE VERDICT OF JESUS CHRIST ON THE SCRIPTURES

In his exegesis of sura 2 verse 159, 'Abduh states that, just as the Jews had altered the Torah so as to reject Christ, so they misinterpreted passages in the Torah that foretold the coming of Muhammad. Jesus did indeed blame the Jewish leaders for their misinterpretation of the Torah and for their human traditions that amounted to nullifying God's word (Mark 7:1–13). Remarkably, however, he never criticized them for changing the text of the Tanakh (what Christians call the "Old Testament"). On the contrary, he showed the greatest respect for this text, insisting that it points to him: "If you believed Moses, you would believe me, for he wrote about me. But since you do not believe what he wrote, how are you going to believe what I say?" (John 5:46–47).

Jesus knew that just as God was unchangeable, so was his word. This was true of the Torah as much as of the Gospel: "Heaven and earth will pass away, but my words will never pass away" (Matt 24:35). Jesus' verdict on the reliability of Scripture is paramount. With the guidance of the Holy Spirit, who revealed them, the message of Scripture becomes plain; otherwise God's decision to reveal his word to us would be pointless. This does not mean that everything in the Bible is easy to understand. The difficult texts summon us to further research, greater humility, and more trust in the divine author of the Scriptures. They should not be allowed to dim our vision of the clarity of the Scriptures' message. Otherwise, we find ourselves in a position where we are not able to see the forest for the trees.

3

GOD

AT THE TIME when the Prophet started preaching the Qur'an (AD 610), the vast majority of Arabs were polytheistic. They believed in one supreme God, *Allah*, but associated with him many other gods and goddesses. Their religion is described in the Qur'an as *shirk*, which literally means "association" or "partnership." Some Arab Jews lived in central Arabia, especially in Yathrib, which became Medina ("the city") after the Prophet settled in this place in 622. A few Christians lived in Mecca, Muhammad's birthplace, such as Waraqa bin Nawfal, the cousin of Muhammad's first wife Khadija.

GOD IN ISLAM

Allah is the only Arabic word for God, used by all Arabs, Christians, and Muslims alike.[10] Thus, contrary to common belief, the word does not designate just "the Muslim God." It is used for God in the Qur'an as well as in all Arabic translations of the Bible. Islamic theology refers to ninety-nine divine names (or attributes) known as "God's most beautiful names." By itself, of course, this commonality of usage does not prove that the *referent* is the same in both religions or that the understanding of God is exactly the same in both traditions: that is a matter still to be discussed.

The Muslim Prophetic Tradition provides two overlapping lists of names.[11] The most important names refer to God's oneness, which is at the core of the Islamic faith. The preaching of the Prophet aimed at convincing his people that they should worship *Allah* and him alone. The first part of the Islamic creed stresses, "There is no god but God." Muslim theologians identify seven main divine attributes (power, science, life, will, speech, hearing, and seeing) which, unlike his creatures, God possesses fully and perfectly.

Apart from God's oneness, the most significant of the divine attributes are those which are exclusive to him. He is *unique* ("there is nothing whatever like unto Him" [42:11]); *eternal*, having neither beginning nor end; *self-existent*, owing his existence to no one other than himself; and *self-sufficient*, having no need whatsoever.

God's names related to his creation depict him as the Creator of the universe (7:54), the Sovereign Lord who has supreme authority and power to do whatever he wants (1:2), the Judge on the day of judgment (1:4), and, last but not least, the Merciful. Each chapter in the Qur'an (except the ninth) starts with the following invocation: "In the Name of God, the Ever-Merciful, the All-Merciful." Especially cherished in the mystical tradition of Islam is the name *al-wadud*, "the loving-kind."

GOD IN CHRISTIANITY

These same divine attributes highlight God's greatness in Christianity, too. Yet God's greatness in the Christian faith is reflected in other attributes that are either missing or do not have the same importance in Islam.

In the Bible, God is unique in the sense that his divine nature is exclusive to him. The first chapter in the Bible makes it clear that human creatures are also unique to the extent that they have been created in God's image: "God created human beings in his own image. In the image of God he created them; male and female he created them" (Gen 1:27 NLT). Christians have sometimes divided over the exact meaning of the expression "image of God," but no Christian tradition tries to do away with the category. By contrast, while the Muslim Prophetic Tradition reports, "God created Adam in his image,"[12] some Muslim theologians have found it difficult to reconcile this saying with God's otherness and therefore have doubted its authenticity. Other Muslims explain it in the sense that human beings, unlike other creatures, possess to some degree certain divine attributes.[13] This interpretation is not far from the way Christians understand God's otherness. A leading Christian theologian has expressed the likeness between our Creator and ourselves in these words:

> Firstly, we human beings are rational and self-conscious. Secondly, we are moral, having a conscience that urges us to do what we perceive to be right. Thirdly, we are creative like our Creator, able to appreciate what is beautiful to the ear and the eye. Fourthly, we are social, able to establish with one

another authentic relationships of love. For God is love, and by making us in his own image, he has given us the capacity to love him and others. Fifthly, we have a spiritual faculty that makes us hunger after God. Thus we are uniquely able to think and to choose, to create, to love, and to worship.[14]

As this quote indicates, love is one of God's paramount attributes: "Whoever does not love does not know God, because God is love" (1 John 4:8). Jesus summed up the teaching of God's law and the prophets in a two-fold command: loving God and loving one's neighbor (Matt 22:34–40).

Another essential name of God in Christianity is "the Father." He is the Father of all human creatures, but especially of his people. Jesus made this name particularly central. The Old Testament compares God to a Father in a few texts. God is described as Israel's Father (Deut 32:6; Jer 3:19; 31:9). Moreover, he promises to have a father-son relationship with the Davidic king (1 Sam 7:14; Ps 89:26). He is "a father to the fatherless, a defender of widows" (Ps 68:5). Jesus, however, names God as "the Father" and frequently addresses him as such throughout his mission. When his disciples ask him to teach them how to pray, he replies, "This, then, is how you should pray: 'Our Father in heaven …'" (Matt 6:9). The fact that our Father is *in heaven* highlights that God is not just a loving God; he is also our sovereign Lord: "This is what the LORD says: 'Heaven is my throne, and the earth is my footstool'" (Isa 66:1). Because God is our Lord, we are accountable to him and he will judge us on the last day. Thus, our heavenly Father is also the universal Lord:

> The words "in the heavens" denote not the place of his abode so much as the authority and power at his command as the creator and ruler of all things. Thus he combines fatherly love with heavenly power, and what his love directs his power is able to perform.[15]

The Qur'an does not explicitly reject the claim that God is the Father, but it denies that Jesus is God's Son. It asserts that God does not have a son because if he did, he would have a female partner: "The very Creator of heavens and earth: How could He have a son when He has no consort? He created all things, and He has full knowledge of all things" (6:101; compare 72:3). This denial assumes that divine fatherhood is identical to human fatherhood, which clearly is not the case. Perhaps this confusion is due to the fact that the Virgin Mary had been given the title "Mother of God" by mainstream Christianity before the rise of Islam.[16] This title was intended to acknowledge Jesus' full divinity, not at all to deify Mary. Whether or not this title is theologically sound, undoubtedly it can be misleading, not least in an Islamic context. The Qur'an specifically rejects the idea of Mary being worshiped with Jesus alongside God. It blames Christian leaders, not Jesus, for teaching that Mary and Jesus are to be worshiped alongside God himself:

> God said, "Jesus, son of Mary, did you ever say to people, 'Adopt me and my mother as two gods in disregard of God Himself?'"
>
> To which he replied, "Glory be to You. It is not in me to say what I have no warrant for. If I had ever said such a thing You would have known it. For You know my innermost being and I do not know Yours." (5:116)

Thus calling God "our Father" is liable to evoke huge misunderstandings among Muslim people. It is therefore extremely important to try to dispel these misunderstandings by spelling out not only what this title means but also what it does not mean.

THE FATHERHOOD OF GOD IN CHRISTIANITY

When we look into the biblical texts that speak of God's fatherhood, we gain a fair idea of what this concept means.

HE IS OUR CREATOR

We owe him our existence and our life, for he has made all of us:

> Yet you, LORD, are our Father.
> We are the clay, you are the potter;
> we are all the work of your hand. (Isa 64:8)

Adam produced his first son, Seth, "in his own likeness, in his own image" (Gen 5:3). This expression is exactly the same as the one used for the creation of humankind by God (Gen 1:26; compare 5:1–2). In other words Adam's relationship with his children mirrored God's relationship with humanity. This indicates that God's relationship with us is similar to what a father's relationship with his sons and daughters ought to be.

HE CARES FOR US

He provides for us and meets our needs, both material and spiritual. In fact, Jesus says that God cares for us much more than our human parents do:

> Which of you, if your son asks for bread, will give him a stone? Or if he asks for a fish, will give him a snake? If you, then, though you are evil, know how to give good gifts to your children, how much more will your Father in heaven give good gifts to those who ask him! (Matt 7:9–11)

HE IS MERCIFUL TO US

Our Creator knows us best, for he has made us. He knows we are weak and has compassion on us:

> As a father has compassion on his children,
> so the LORD has compassion on those who fear him;
> for he knows how we are formed;
> he remembers that we are dust. (Ps 103:13–14)

29

HE DISCIPLINES US

Our Maker is also our Teacher. He helps us to grow morally and spiritually. When necessary he disciplines us:

Have you completely forgotten this word of encouragement that addresses you as a father addresses his son? It says,

"My son, do not make light of the Lord's discipline,
     and do not lose heart when he rebukes you,
because the Lord disciplines the one he loves,
     and he chastens everyone he accepts as his son."

Endure hardship as discipline; God is treating you as his children. For what children are not disciplined by their father? ... [Our human fathers] disciplined us for a little while as they thought best; but God disciplines us for our good, in order that we may share in his holiness. (Heb 12:5, 7, 10)

All these attributes and actions associated with God's fatherhood in the Bible are acceptable from an Islamic point of view. This may not be the case with the following attributes.

HE IS OUR DIVINE FRIEND

Because God is our heavenly Father we can have a close and intimate relationship with him: "Have you not just called to me: 'My Father, my friend from my youth, will you always be angry?'" (Jer 3:4). Jesus calls his disciples his friends and explains to them that this friendship implies that they will obey his commands:

> You are my friends if you do what I command. I no longer call you servants, because a servant does not know his master's business. Instead, I have called you friends, for everything that I learned from my Father I have made known to you. (John 15:14–15)

Clearly God is no ordinary friend; he is our Creator. Our friendship with him is not between equals. So also our relationship with Jesus: we must obey his commands, as Jesus makes clear to his disciples. In this respect the "friendship" is not perfectly reciprocal. The Old Testament, the New Testament, and the Qur'an alike describe Abraham as God's friend (2 Chr 20:7; Isa 41:8; Jas 2:23; Qur'an 4:125); they do not refer to God as Abraham's friend. Transparently, however, the Bible presents God as the best "friend" any sinner can ever have, even if the terminology only rarely runs in that direction. In mainstream Islam, not everyone can enjoy God's friendship; only prophets and saints have this privilege. The New Testament tells us that God extends his "friendship" to all human beings who truly confess Jesus as Lord.

HE LOVES US

God loves us all regardless of who we are (John 3:16; 1 John 4:8, 16). Love is more comprehensive and demanding than mercy. Merciful people are willing to help those in need, but they are not necessarily committed to love them in a personal, enduring, and possibly costly relationship. Jesus explained to his disciples what love ultimately means: "Greater love has no one than this: to lay down one's life for one's friends" (John 15:13). Jesus' self-sacrifice on the cross demonstrates the extent of his love for his disciples.

HE IS OUR SAVIOR

We have all disobeyed God's law and gone astray. We have not given our Creator the honor that is due him:

> "A son honors his father, and a slave his master. If I am a father, where is the honor due me? If I am a master, where is the respect due me?" says the LORD Almighty. (Mal 1:6)

We deserve God's punishment. Because God is a loving God, however, he wants to forgive our sins and to save us. He saved the people of Israel from death when Pharaoh's army pursued them. In doing so, he revealed himself as their Redeeming Father:

> But you are our Father,
>   though Abraham does not know us
>   or Israel acknowledge us;
> you, LORD, are our Father,
>   our Redeemer from of old is your name.
>   (Isa 63:16)

WHAT GOD'S FATHERHOOD
DOES NOT MEAN

Divine fatherhood is not identical to human fatherhood. By saying that God is our Father in heaven, Jesus indicates that if God can be likened to human fathers in some ways, he is also different from them in other ways. God the Father is different from human fathers in many ways:

1. God's divine nature is exclusive to him. We have the same human nature as our human fathers, but we do not have the same nature as our divine Father. The heavenly Father shares his divine essence with none of his creatures.

2. God has no gender and no partner. He is beyond sexual differentiation that characterizes humankind and other creatures. If in the Bible he is persistently addressed as "Father" but not as "Mother," it is because of analogical arguments.

3. God is perfect and self-sufficient whereas human fathers and mothers are dependent, and, this side of the fall, fallible and sinful. At the same time, his love for us is much greater than any parental love.

4. God is Spirit (John 4:24). He is not a material being. He is not located in one place; his presence is everywhere.

5. God is to be honored and worshiped whereas human parents are to be honored (Exod 20:12) but not worshiped.

6. There are many human fathers but only one heavenly Father: "Do we not all have one Father? Did not one God create us?" (Mal 2:10).

7. Human fathers have a limited number of children. Insofar as he is the Creator, God is the Father of *all* human beings; insofar as God's role as Father refers to his relationship with those he has redeemed, he is the Father of *all* believers.

This last point calls for a further reflection. Because we have been made by God, we can all call God "our Father": we have all been made in his image. This means that we are all equally human in God's sight, equally God's image-bearers, regardless of our ethnic, social, or religious backgrounds. As human beings we are brothers and sisters. Especially in the New Testament writings, however, God is addressed as Father in function of his peculiar relationship with the people he redeems in Christ. They become "brothers" and "sisters" in a community of redeemed believers—even though they are drawn from every ethnicity, nation, and language (e.g., Rev 5:9–10). In the fourth century, Augustine rightly commented, "Before this Father, the rich and the poor are brothers; before this Father, the master and the slave are brothers; before this Father, the army general and the simple soldier are brothers."[17]

Thus God's fatherhood is similar, not identical, to human fatherhood. In some respects, human fatherhood mirrors divine fatherhood; in others it does not. God's immanence, in particular his likeness with human beings, must always be held together with his transcendence. We must not abuse his overwhelming love for us by being so self-obsessed that we fail to recognize the differences between God and ourselves, who bear his image. On the contrary, his love for us should deepen our love for him, our obedience to his word, and our worship of him. In instructing us to call God our Father, Jesus discloses how privileged we are as human beings. This privilege carries with it a moral responsibility:

> If he [Jesus] commands us to call God "Father" in our prayer, he commands you to model your life upon the Father in heaven. He commands this even more explicitly when he says, "Be perfect, therefore, as your heavenly Father is perfect" (Matt 5:48).[18]

It is our privilege as human beings to be able to reflect God's fatherly character to some degree, especially with our children. But in the final analysis God remains an incomparable Father. Here is the point where Christianity and Islam converge. Jesus has such a high view of God's uniqueness—and his own—that he goes as far as to instruct his disciples not to let people call them "masters" or "teachers" and not to call anyone father, for they have one Father, God, and one Teacher, himself:

> You are not to be called "Rabbi," for you have only one Teacher, and you are all brothers. And do not call anyone on earth "father," for you have one Father, and he is in heaven. Nor are you to be called instructors, for you have one Instructor, the Messiah. (Matt 23:8–10)

Here Jesus is not literally asking his disciples to refrain from addressing human beings by their titles. His concern is much deeper. We should never forget that humans are all fallible and that God is the source of all authority and all knowledge. Therefore we should always take a critical look at human teaching and leadership. Above all, we should assign our ultimate loyalty and gratitude to God and to the One who revealed him to us as "our Father in heaven."

Although he is our Creator and Lord, God has revealed himself to us as our loving Father.

4

JESUS CHRIST

T HE PROPHET MUHAMMAD preached the Qur'an to polytheist Arabs, hence the emphasis of his message on God's oneness, which is at the heart of Islamic faith. By contrast, Jesus carried out his mission among the Jewish people who, since the time of Moses, believed that God is one: "Hear, O Israel: 'The LORD our God, the LORD is one'" (Deut 6:4). Therefore his message was focused not so much on God's oneness as on who God is: "our Father in heaven." During his mission he made an even more extraordinary claim that upset many people, especially the Jewish establishment: he is God's one and only Son (John 1:14, 18). He enjoys a unique relationship with his Father. His mission was precisely to make it possible for us to model our relationship with our heavenly Father on his (though his own uniqueness is never called into question):

> All things have been committed to me by my Father. No one knows the Son except the Father, and no one knows the Father except the Son and those to whom the Son chooses to reveal him. (Matt 11:27)

Sometimes Jesus calls God "Father" without even using the word "God." He invokes God most frequently and most naturally as "the Father," "my Father," and "your Father." He never associates himself with his disciples in addressing

God as "our (common) Father." Jesus paid with his life for the claim he made about who he is. The Jewish tribunal condemned him to death as a blasphemer (Mark 14:61–64). After he was raised from the dead he declared to his followers: "I am ascending to my Father and your Father, to my God and your God" (John 20:17). The resurrection of Jesus from the dead is, among other things, the way God vindicated him and endorsed his claim to be unique among the prophets.

WHAT IS SO UNIQUE ABOUT JESUS?

Let us now consider briefly other aspects of Jesus' uniqueness as they appear in the Gospels. Because of his humble character (Matt 11:29), Jesus did not openly and directly speak, let alone boast, about his divinity. He never said, "I am God," not least because such a formulation might mislead people to think that he was undermining God's oneness. Nevertheless, he did say such things as "I and the Father are one" (John 10:30) and "Don't you know me, Philip, even after I have been among you such a long time? Anyone who has seen me has seen the Father" (John 14:9). Again, he claims more than pre-existence but takes on the name of God: "Very truly I tell you," Jesus declares, "before Abraham was born, I am!" (John 8:58). Jesus can speak about the uniqueness of his own "sonship" (e.g., John 10:34–36), including the astonishing claim that he, as the Son, while functionally subordinate to his Father, nevertheless does all that the Father does, while the Father is determined that all should honor the Son even as they honor the Father (John 5:16–30). Certainly the first witnesses can either address him as God (note Thomas's "My Lord and my God!" [John 20:28]) or speak of him as God (John 1:1). Moreover, the Gospels are full of other indicators of his divine nature.

JESUS' BIRTH

Unlike all human beings, Jesus had no biological father. The Qur'an acknowledges the virginal conception of Jesus, which is why Jesus is often referred to as "the son of Mary." However, the Qur'an sees in this miracle simply a sign pointing to God's unlimited power (21:91). The creation of Jesus is explicitly compared in the Qur'an to that of Adam (3:59). Adam too was created directly by God, but this does not make him God's son.

According to the Bible, Adam is also in a sense "the son of God" (Luke 3:37) because of the way he was created. Yet we must make a distinction between Adam and Jesus. Because Adam was the first human being, his coming into existence had to be the result of God's direct creative act, but this was not so with Jesus. Adam, of course, has no claimed pre-existence;[19] Jesus does. Adam was never worshiped as God; Jesus was. What is equally significant about Jesus' birth are the names that God himself gave him after he was conceived in Mary's womb. He was to be named Jesus "because he will save his people from their sins" (Matt 1:21) and Immanuel, "which means 'God with us'" (Matt 1:23). These two names sum up Jesus' identity and mission. The angel Gabriel told Mary that her son would also be called "the Son of the Most High" and that "his kingdom will never end" (Luke 1:32–33): indeed, sometimes "son of God" as applied to Jesus shows him to be the unique messianic king in David's line (note how 2 Sam 7:14 and Ps 2 are applied to Jesus in the New Testament, especially in Hebrews: see further below).

JESUS' TITLES

Both the Qur'an and the Bible give Jesus three titles that are exclusive to him: God's Word (3:39, 45; 4:171), the Messiah (3:45), and God's Spirit (4:171). The Qur'an does not explain the meaning of these titles. Muslim scholars have suggested various interpretations, all of which fall short of their biblical meanings.[20]

God's Word

Jesus is God's eternal Word, revealed in the form of a human being. He is the revelation of God in a human person in a sense that is similar to God's word being revealed in a book:

> In the beginning was the Word, and the Word was with God, and the Word was God. He was with God in the beginning. Through him all things were made; without him nothing was made that has been

made. … The Word became flesh and made his
dwelling among us. (John 1:1–3, 14a)

Christians use the word "incarnation" to refer to God's
becoming a human being through his Son in the person
of Jesus Christ, without giving up his divine nature. The
Bible points to Jesus Christ as God's ultimate and perfect
revelation.

The Messiah

The Messiah, or the Christ, is the king God promised to
raise up as one of David's descendants (2 Sam 7). This king
would enjoy a father-son relationship with God and would
make all the peoples of the earth his subjects (Ps 2). King
David called him his Lord (Ps 110:1). The prophet Micah
identified Bethlehem as the place of his birth, describing his
origins as ancient and eternal (Mic 5:2). Isaiah announced
that the Messiah would preside over an eternal kingdom
of peace and justice (Isa 9:7).

Jesus knew himself to be the long-awaited Messiah.
However, he was not the kind of Messiah his people were
expecting, that is, a political king. He was the Messiah
foretold by the prophets, the saving King who would
conquer the world through his death and resurrection
(Matt 16:13–28). Following his resurrection, Jesus ascended
to heaven, where God enthroned him as Lord of the
world. He now reigns over everything in heaven and earth

(Matt 28:18–20), even though that reign is still contested. One day he will return in glory, and his lordship will then be recognized by everyone (1 Cor 15:20–28).

God's Spirit

The Bible speaks of Adam as "a pattern of the one to come," namely, Jesus Christ (Rom 5:14). There is both a parallel and a contrast between Adam and Christ. Adam was the first human being to disobey God whereas Christ remained sinless. Unlike Adam who was given life when God created him from clay (Gen 2:7; compare Qur'an 15:26–29), the resurrected Christ gives new life to those who believe in him: "So it is written, 'The first man Adam became a living being'; the last Adam, a life-giving spirit" (1 Cor 15:45). Jesus is "the last Adam" insofar as his mission consisted in saving humanity from sin and creating a new and redeemed humanity.

JESUS' MISSION

The message Jesus preached is known in the Qur'an as the *injil*. Because this word derives from Greek, its meaning is not known to Muslims. The Arabic equivalent would be *bushra* or "good news." The good news of the gospel is that God has become in the person of Jesus Christ, through his death and resurrection, "the Savior of the world" (John 4:42). Our salvation depends on his unexpected and costly love, not on our merits and good works.

From an Islamic perspective, miracles are meant to authenticate the mission of God's prophets. The Qur'an ascribes several miracles to Jesus, including healing the blind and the leper, raising the dead, creating birds from clay, and miraculously feeding his people (5:110–15).[21] According to the Gospels, however, Jesus' miracles had another dimension: they were signs that pointed to and disclosed who Jesus was. Before Jesus healed the blind man he said, "I am the light of the world" (John 9:5). Before he raised Lazarus from the dead he said, "I am the resurrection and the life. Anyone who believes in me will live, even though they die" (John 11:25). After he fed the crowd he said, "I am the bread of life. Whoever comes to me will never go hungry, and whoever believes in me will never be thirsty" (John 6:35). What is unique about Jesus is not the miracles he worked as much as the claims he made in connection with these miracles. No prophet has ever made such claims about himself. Some Muslims have been particularly impressed with Jesus' ability to create and to raise people from the dead. Is not God the only Creator and the only One who gives life and death (2:258; 30:50)? The Qur'anic text specifies that it was "by God's leave" that Jesus worked miracles, but the question remains, "What entitled Jesus to make such claims?"

According to the Qur'an, God strengthened Jesus with (literally) "the Holy Spirit" during his mission (2:87, 253; 5:110). Muslim scholars understand the Holy Spirit to refer to the angel Gabriel for fear of undermining God's oneness. The Arabic Bible uses exactly the same expression for the Holy Spirit, the third person of the Holy Trinity. Jesus was filled with the Holy Spirit during his mission (John 3:34). He spoke about the Holy Spirit as the one who would succeed him when he himself had left the disciples to return to his Father—another person, like himself, to help them (John 14–16). He would send him to the disciples to remain with them forever. He refers to him as "the Spirit of truth" whose mission is to guide his disciples into all the truth (John 16:13). The Holy Spirit came upon the disciples ten days after Jesus ascended to heaven (Acts 2).

JESUS' SINLESS LIFE

The Bible provides many passages that affirm Jesus' utter sinlessness (e.g., 2 Cor 5:21; Heb 7:27; 1 John 3:5). The Qur'an affirms the same truth. It tells us that when Gabriel appeared to Mary he told her that she would be the mother of "a holy son" (19:19). The Islamic Prophetic Tradition confirms Jesus' uniqueness in this respect: "There is none among the offspring of Adam but Satan touches it. A child, therefore, cries loudly at the time of birth because of the touch of Satan, except Mary and her child."[22] If all human beings are hit by evil at their birth except Jesus, what does this exception say about him? The New Testament not only highlights that Jesus was absolutely sinless; it also specifies that it is precisely his moral perfection that made him fit to offer his life as a sacrifice for sin:

I write this to you so that you will not sin. But if anybody does sin, we have an advocate with the Father—Jesus Christ, the Righteous One. He is the atoning sacrifice for our sins, and not only for ours but also for the sins of the whole world. (1 John 2:1–2; compare Heb 7:26–28)

JESUS' CLAIMS

1. *He has the authority to forgive sins.* No one has the right to forgive people their sins—no one, that is, except God. This belief is shared by Jews, Christians, and Muslims (see Qur'an 3:135). One day a paralyzed man, lying on a mat, was carried before Jesus. Everyone expected that Jesus would heal him, but instead Jesus said to the man, "Son, your sins are forgiven." The teachers of the law were indignant. In order to convince his critics that he had the power to forgive sins, Jesus turned to the sick man and said, "Get up, take your mat and go home!" To the amazement of the crowd, the man got up, took his mat, and walked out in front of them (Mark 2:1–12). Would God have given Jesus the power to heal the sick man if he had no right to forgive the man's sins? Jesus granted forgiveness of sins to people in other circumstances (Luke 7:36–50; John 8:1–11). The question is, "Why did God give the authority to forgive sins to no other prophet than Jesus?" If it is true that in the ultimate sense only God can forgive sins, then Jesus' forgiving sins (which he validates by the confirming miracle) speaks of more than vague uniqueness, but of his very identity as God.

49

2. *His authority is above God's law.* The law of Moses prohibited the Jewish people from working on the Sabbath. This was one of the Ten Commandments (Exod 20:8–11). Yet Jesus declared one day, "The Sabbath was made for man, not man for the Sabbath. So the Son of Man [Jesus] is Lord even of the Sabbath" (Mark 2:27). On another occasion, Jesus challenged the continuing validity of the food laws, a point the evangelist Mark well understands, for he comments, "In saying this, Jesus declared all foods clean" (Mark 7:19). More broadly, although Jesus invariably treats Old Testament law as truly the word of God, he commonly speaks and acts as if that law is something that points toward him, something that *he and he alone fulfills* (e.g., Matt 5:17; Luke 24:44–47; John 5:46).

3. *He is God's new temple.* One day Jesus was appalled by the trading carried on inside the temple in Jerusalem. He turned everyone out. The Jewish authorities were furious. They demanded that Jesus explain his actions: "What sign can you show us to prove your authority to do all this?" Jesus' response was rather enigmatic: "Destroy this temple, and I will raise it again in three days" (John 2:19). By these words Jesus indicated that he would rise from the dead on the third day after his crucifixion. The temple was the great meeting place between God and his people. It was the place of sacrifice, the place of atonement. By claiming to be the temple, Jesus was announcing that he himself would become the great meeting place between God and his people. Because of his death and resurrection, people

would then worship God through him. Shortly after his resurrection his first disciples worshiped him as "Lord and God" (John 20:28; compare Matt 28:16–17).

4. *He is the Judge on the day of judgment.* Jesus claims to be the judge on the day of judgment (Matt 7:21–23; 25:31–34; John 5:24–27), thus asserting for himself a role that belongs to God alone. Islam agrees that final judgment belongs to God: the Qur'an describes God as "the King on the Day of Judgment" (1:4). The fact that Jesus identifies himself as the one who will call people to give account for their lives is most significant.

A careful reading of the Gospels leaves us with no doubt about the uniqueness of Jesus in both his person and his mission. This uniqueness is encapsulated by his title "Son of God." Christians are compelled by the biblical evidence to believe in the Trinitarian God (the loving Father, the saving Son, and the sanctifying Spirit) who is over us, with us, and within us.

A CHRISTIAN RESPONSE
TO ISLAMIC OBJECTIONS
ABOUT JESUS

We have suggested in the previous section that the Qur'an rightly rejects a misconception of the Trinity as being God, Mary, and Jesus (5:116). If the Qur'an, like the Bible, is to be interpreted by itself and according to its historical context, this means that some other Qur'anic texts denying the so-called Christian Trinity are best understood as inveighing against the same construction of God-Mary-Jesus: God is not three (gods) (4:171); Jesus is not the third of three (gods) (5:76); Christ is not the son of God (9:30); God is not Christ (5:17, 72); and God does neither beget nor is he begotten (112:3). What the Qur'an actually denies in such passages is the tritheism of God-Mary-Jesus that was perceived to be a Christian form of Arab polytheism. In such polytheism God was believed to have female companions (6:102; 72:3) as well as daughters, three of whom are actually mentioned by name (53:19–20; compare 16:57; 43:19; 53:27).

In the centuries following the circulation of the Qur'an, Muslim theologians also rejected the biblical understanding of the Trinity on the grounds that it too undermines God's oneness. They put forward several arguments:

"THE CHRISTIAN DOCTRINE DOES NOT MAKE SENSE"

"Either God is one or he is three. Either Jesus Christ is God or he is a man. You cannot have it both ways. The word 'Trinity' is not even found in the Bible."

This rationalistic argument is rather surprising as Islam is not a rationalistic religion. *Islam* means submitting ourselves, including our minds, to God. Faith consists in trusting God and his word even when his revelation is beyond our understanding. When Muslims say *Allahu akbar*, do they not mean that God is far greater than us, including our human rationality? It is true that the word "Trinity" is a theological word that Christians have chosen to express their belief about God and that the word is not in the Bible, but its meaning is consistent with the Bible's teaching. The word *tawḥid* (monotheism) is not in the Qur'an either, but its theological content is indisputable among Muslims. In the Bible the linking of Father, Son, and Holy Spirit is not uncommon. For instance, before he left his disciples, Jesus commissioned them to be his witnesses with the following words:

> All authority in heaven and on earth has been given to me. Therefore go and make disciples of all nations, baptizing them in the name of the Father and of the Son and of the Holy Spirit, and teaching them to obey everything I have commanded you. And surely I am with you always, to the very end of the age. (Matt 28:18–20)

"IT IS UNFITTING FOR GOD TO BECOME A HUMAN BEING"

Some Muslim scholars argue that it is simply unbecoming for God to humble himself to the point of becoming a human being. But both Muslims and Christians believe that God is sovereign and free to do whatever he wants, so as God's servants we have no right to challenge our Creator even if what he reveals to us is difficult to believe. Do not Muslims elsewhere assert, "He cannot be questioned for His acts, but they will be questioned for theirs" (21:23)? Who are we, then, to assert that it is demeaning for God to

53

become a human being (43:81)? If we apply human standards to God, we will make him into our own image. If God sovereignly decides to humble himself, who are we to challenge him? Did he not create man and woman in his own image (Gen 1:26–27)? May this not make it possible for him to take possession of his image and to dwell in it, so to speak? Does not the Qur'an say that God appointed humankind as his *caliph*, that is, his representative on earth (2:30)? Since God created us with such dignity, it is neither inconceivable nor degrading for him to identify with his human creatures.

"JESUS IS GOD'S SON ONLY IN A SYMBOLIC SENSE"

Some Muslim scholars accept that Jesus is a special prophet, but then every prophet is special in his own way. They argue that Christians should not take literally the title "Son of God" given to him metaphorically in the Gospels.[23] After all, they point out, the Bible itself applies this expression to Adam (Luke 3:38), angels (Job 1:6), Israel (Deut 14:1), Solomon (2 Sam 7:14), and Jesus' own disciples (Luke 6:35).

This argument does not take into account that Jesus is said to be God's *one and only* Son (John 3:16, 18). It does not do justice to the texts that highlight the uniqueness of Jesus' birth, names, mission, claims, and resurrection. The resurrection of Jesus Christ, followed by his ascension to heaven and enthronement by God, is an unparalleled event in human history.

It is therefore very important to dispel some misunderstandings. The divine sonship of Jesus is neither physical nor temporal. It is to be understood neither literally nor symbolically but spiritually. This means the following:

1. Jesus is not God's Son because he was conceived miraculously in Mary's womb, but the other way round: Jesus was conceived this way because he is God's eternal Son.

2. God created Jesus' human nature when he was conceived in Mary's womb. This means that as well as being divine, Jesus is fully a human being, and his Qur'anic name "Jesus, son of Mary" is fully justified.

3. God cannot be reduced to the person of the Son alone. While it is correct that *Christ is God* (by virtue of his divine nature), it is not true that *God is Christ*, as if God were exhausted in Christ. God is the Father, the Son, and the Holy Spirit.

4. The incarnation of the Son of God does not at all mean making a man into a god. The incarnation is exactly the opposite of the deification of a man. The former refers to the self-abasement of God, whereas the latter is about the elevation of a man to God's rank. Certainly God did not *take* Jesus as his Son.

55

5. The divine and the human natures have been united in the one person of Jesus Christ. Christians worship the person of Christ and not his divine or human nature. This union neither deifies human nature nor humanizes divine nature. The two natures remain distinct, unconfused, and unmixed. Therefore, in no way do Christians associate in their worship the Creator with what is created.

6. God is not one and three from the same point of view, which would be a contradiction in terms. He is one nature and three persons. The Holy Trinity is about the loving God, his eternal Word, and his living Spirit.

7. The expression "son of God" has (as we have noted) a variety of referents in the Bible, depending on the context. In the same way it has a variety of overtones even when it is quite clearly referring to Jesus. In some New Testament passages it functions to assert that Jesus is the true, long-awaited, Davidic king, the ultimate fulfillment of passages such as 2 Samuel 7:11b–16, Psalm 2, and Isaiah 9.

5

SIN AND FORGIVENESS

JUDAISM, CHRISTIANITY, AND Islam teach that human beings are morally accountable to their Creator and Judge. They are expected to comply with God's revealed law. If they fail, they commit sin. In all three religions God is known as a forgiving Lord. This section looks into human sin, divine forgiveness, and the way they relate to each other in Christianity and Islam.[24]

SIN IN CHRISTIANITY
AND ISLAM

THE DEFINITION OF SIN

Sin is disobeying God's commands (1 John 3:4). It disrupts our relationship with our Creator, our fellow human beings, the environment, and ourselves. In Christianity, God is not only displeased with us when we sin, he is also grieved and personally affected. Ultimately our offense offends the law-giver himself, our heavenly Father (Ps 51:4; Luke 15:18). In Islam, the sinner does wrong to himself (65:1). God remains unaffected by our actions since he is far above his human creatures.

Islamic teaching explains sin in terms of people's ignorance, weakness, or misjudgment. While all this may be true, the biblical diagnosis of sin goes deeper into the human heart. Sin has to do with our innermost attitude toward God. We want to live our lives our way instead of acknowledging our dependence on him. We want to be our own judge in deciding what is right and wrong instead of trusting him. This is the root of our wrongdoing and sinful behavior.

THE SERIOUSNESS AND PENALTY OF SIN

Mainstream Islam considers all sins to be serious, whether they are hidden or uncovered. Indeed they represent grievous violations of the law of God, who is so generous with us and who is our supreme Judge. People will be punished for their sins in the afterlife unless God decides to forgive them. There is one sin that God will never forgive (unless people repent): polytheism (4:48). If people are guilty of this sin, they will certainly suffer eternal punishment.

Mu'tazili theology (an alternative expression of Islamic orthodoxy) divides sin into major sins and minor sins. Only major sins are serious since one major sin will send a person to hell if one does not repent of it. Major sins are not all known to people. This ignorance is meant to be a deterrent: we are more likely to keep away from any sin if we know it might be a major one. The Prophetic Tradition lists seven major sins, but this is by no means an exhaustive list.[25] Major sins include polytheism (22:31), apostasy, adultery, robbery, witchcraft, murder (4:93), consuming the property of an orphan (4:10), usury (2:275), running away from a battle (8:15), slandering a married Muslim woman (24:23), rebellion against one's parents, lying, taking false oaths, giving false testimony, drinking wine, and abusing or despairing of God's mercy.

The penalty for sin in the Bible is physical and spiritual death in this life and the next. God commanded Adam and Eve not to eat from "the tree of the knowledge of good and evil," for he said, "when you eat from it you will certainly die" (Gen 2:17; compare Rom 6:23). We do not find this solemn warning in the Qur'anic story of Adam and Eve's disobedience. Like the Bible, the Qur'an tells us that God expelled Adam and Eve from paradise following their disobedience (Gen 2:23–24; Qur'an 2:36; 7:24; 20:123), but Muslim scholars do not understand this banishment necessarily in terms of punishment. In fact both Adam and Eve repented and God forgave them.

THE SCOPE OF SIN

Muslim theologians often object to the Christian doctrine of "original sin." They argue that each person is individually responsible for their conduct, as the Qur'an says: "No soul shall bear the burden of another soul" (6:164). Islamic teaching claims that people are born sinless. They are sinners but not sinful.

Christians contend that human beings are all members of the same human family. When our parents Adam and Eve disobeyed God's command, their sin had serious repercussions not only for themselves but also for their offspring. The unprovoked murder of Adam's son Abel by his brother Cain is a poignant demonstration of this (Gen 4:1–16;

compare Qur'an 5:30–34). From a Christian perspective, when people are born, they are oriented toward evil; they are not morally neutral. Their sinful nature leads them to commit sin. Jesus explains that what we do reflects who we are in our uttermost being: "For it is from within, out of a person's heart that evil thoughts come—sexual immorality, theft, murder, adultery, greed, malice, deceit, lewdness, envy, slander, arrogance and folly" (Mark 7:21–22).

The Qur'an says that "the soul is prone to evil" (12:53). Human beings are perverse and thankless (70:19), contentious (18:54), and rebellious (96:6). As we have already seen, another Muslim prophetic saying asserts that all human beings (except Jesus and Mary) are struck by Satan as soon as they are born. Furthermore, the Qur'an highlights the universality of sin. We are all sinners and deserve God's judgment: "If God were to treat people according to their evildoing, no creature would escape His punishment, but he gives them a fixed respite" (16:61). In other words, as regards the extent and the depth of sin in humanity, Christian doctrine and at least some texts in Qur'anic teaching are not as far apart as they are often assumed to be by both Christians and Muslims. Nevertheless the power of evil and its manifold outworking in humanity, including among religious people, appear more clearly in the Bible than in the Qur'an.

THE REPARATION OF SIN

Good works are expected from Christians and Muslims. The role of good works, however, is not the same in the two religions. In Islam, good works have an atoning effect; they make up for evil deeds as "the good deeds remove the evil ones" (11:114). The first beneficiaries of good actions are their authors.

This is not so in the Christian faith. We are not in a position to redeem our wrongdoing (Isa 64:6; Rom 3:20). Our good works indicate that our faith makes a significant difference in our lives. Our reformed life shows the reality of God at work in our heart. Like a living tree, genuine faith naturally produces good fruit: "As the body without the spirit is dead, so faith without deeds is dead" (Jas 2:26; Eph 2:8–10).

FORGIVENESS IN ISLAM

Divine sovereignty, justice, and mercy are all relevant to divine pardon in Islam as well as in Christianity. Muslims generally emphasize one of these three attributes, which determines how they conceive of God's forgiveness. These attributes characterize the three main schools in Islamic thought: Ash'arism, Mu'tazilism, and Sufism.

GOD IS SOVEREIGN: HE WILL
EVENTUALLY FORGIVE ALL MUSLIMS

The majority of Muslim theologians consider that God's highest attribute is his sovereignty. It comes before his mercy and justice. He has the right to do whatever he likes: "He will forgive whom He will and He will punish whom He will" (2:284; compare 3:129; 5:20, 43; 48:14). His forgiveness depends exclusively on his free decision. We already said that polytheism is the only unforgivable sin: "God does not forgive that partners be associated with Him, but He forgives any other sin to whom He pleases" (4:48).

As monotheistic believers, Muslims are not guilty of committing the only unforgivable sin. Hence all their sins are forgivable in principle. Will God forgive disobedient and unrepentant Muslims their sins on the day of judgment? No one knows the answer because no one can anticipate God's decision. He may forgive, and they will go to paradise; or he may not, and they will go to hell. God will disclose his final verdict only on the day when he will judge everyone.

God is merciful as well. God's mercy will be demonstrated in the fact that he will not condemn disobedient Muslims to eternal punishment. After they have paid for their sins, they will come out of hell and will go to paradise where they will enjoy eternal happiness with their fellow Muslims.[26] On the day of judgment, God's mercy will also be shown when he accepts the Prophet's intercession for his community. Muhammad will ask God's forgiveness for those Muslims who need it most: "My intercession will be for members of my Nation that have committed major sins."[27]

Muhammad's intercession is based on his personal privileges: he is the last Prophet (33:40), and God has forgiven his sins already (48:2). As a result of the Prophet's intercession, God will forgive many Muslims their sins. They will either go directly to paradise, or the time of their stay in hell will be shortened. Thus God's mercy will take the form of a temporary punishment for unrighteous Muslims.[28]

God's justice will mean eternal happiness for righteous Muslims and eternal punishment for non-Muslims.

GOD IS JUST: HE WILL FORGIVE
ONLY OBEDIENT MUSLIMS

Mu'tazili theologians advocate an alternative view of God's pardon. They believe God's key attribute is justice, which comes before his mercy and his sovereignty. On the day of resurrection, God will judge everyone according to his perfect justice. Muslims will not be favored because of their faith (99:7–8; compare 10:61; 21:47; 34:3).

According to Mu'tazili teaching, not only polytheism but also major sins are unforgivable unless people repent from them. God's justice would be compromised if he were to forgive major sins. People must avoid committing sin, especially major ones, if they entertain any hope of going to paradise: "If you keep away from major [sins], We will pardon your [minor] sins and introduce you [to Paradise] through a gate of great honor" (4:31). One major sin that has not been repented from will earn the person eternal punishment. Unlike major sins, minor sins can be redeemed with good deeds as "the good deeds remove the evil ones" (11:114). Provided people have not committed any major sin, God will forgive their minor sins, even if they have not been repented from, as this does not undermine his justice.

The belief about temporary punishment in hell is rejected by Mu'tazili theologians. They claim it has no basis in the Qur'an, and the Hadith narratives about it are unreliable. For the same reasons, they reject the belief that the Prophet will intercede for unrepentant Muslims who have committed major sins. God would deny his justice if he were to forgive major sins.

God's overriding justice in Mu'tazilite theology means that Muslims have no guarantee whatsoever that they will go to paradise. If they deserve God's punishment, they will stay in hell forever. However, their suffering will be less painful than that of non-Muslims.

GOD IS MERCIFUL: HE WILL
EVENTUALLY FORGIVE ALL PEOPLE

Sufism, or Islamic mysticism, represents an important trend within the Muslim world. In Sufism, God's major attribute is mercy. Ibn 'Arabi (d. 638/1240) considers mercy to be God's defining attribute. He is "the most merciful of those who are merciful" (7:151) and "the best of those who are merciful" (23:109). His mercy embraces "all things" (7:156), and "He has prescribed mercy upon Himself" (6:12, 54). God's mercy is all-inclusive; when it is expressed in forgiving people their sins, it has no limitations whatsoever: "Say: 'O My servants who have transgressed against their souls! Despair not of God's mercy. God forgives all sins, for He is the All-Forgiving, the All-Merciful'" (39:53).

For Ibn 'Arabi, this text clearly shows that no sin is beyond God's pardon, not even polytheism. It also indicates that God's forgiveness is unconditional: it does not depend on people's repentance. Finally, it is most comprehensive as it includes everyone. God's justice will be satisfied on the day of resurrection when unrepentant Muslims and non-Muslims will be sent to hell. However, God's mercy would be denied if their punishment were eternal. His mercy is such that it will necessarily bring people's suffering to an end. Disobedient Muslims and all other monotheistic believers will come out of hell and will go to paradise. Everyone else will stay in hell, but hell itself will be transformed. It will no longer be a place of enduring suffering; instead it will become a place where people will enjoy a different kind of happiness forever.

Ibn 'Arabi believes that the Prophet is the mediator of God's universal mercy: "We have sent you as a mercy to the worlds" (21:107; compare 34:28). Muhammad was the last prophet in terms of his physical appearance in the sixth century AD, but he is also the first prophet as his existence predates Adam's creation. In terms of eminence, Muhammad is the first prophet, and all prophets have been his deputies. They have been sent to their respective peoples while he was sent to humankind as a whole. All prophets are sinless, and Muhammad is *the* Prophet. The sins of humankind are attributed to him as he is their leader and representative. His "past sins" are the sins of the people from Adam to his own time, and his "future sins" are the sins of the people from then to the day of resurrection. God will forgive Muhammad's past and future sins (48:2) in response to his intercession on behalf of his nation, in other words, humankind. God's universal amnesty in the world to come will demonstrate that "his favor is indeed overwhelming" (2:105).

FORGIVENESS IN CHRISTIANITY

Ibn 'Arabi's emphasis on God's unconditional and universal mercy is initially strikingly similar to the Christian doctrine of God's love. Ibn 'Arabi's belief, however, about the key role of the Prophet as the mediator of God's love is in sharp conflict with the Bible, which assigns this role to Jesus Christ (John 3:16; 1 Tim 2:5; confer 1 John 4:8). More striking yet is the ground on which the God of the Bible forgives sin: he does so not because he is "merciful" such that he is willing to overlook sin, but because in the person of his Son he pays the penalty for sin. The perfection both of God's holiness and of God's grace is thus maintained: the holy God demands that sin be punished, and then, in the person of his Son, bears that punishment himself. The New Testament presents Jesus Christ as the only qualified mediator between God and humankind, and this for three reasons: he is the only sinless human being who ever existed (John 10:46; Heb 7:26; 9:14); he died for our sins (1 John 2:1–2; Heb 2:17–18); and (as we have seen) he is God's eternal Son, not only a prophet. The difference between the Bible and the theology of Ibn 'Arabi at this point could scarcely be greater—and in the matter of forgiveness of sins, Ibn 'Arabi, with his emphasis on God's universal mercy, represents, among Muslims, the closest approach to Christianity. The majority Muslim vision and practice insists that, however merciful God is, sinners must atone for their own sins by their own works.

Jesus' redeeming mission was predicted by the Old Testament prophets (e.g., Isa 53:4–12; see also Matt 26:54; Luke 24:44–47). He died on the cross as "the Lamb of God, who takes away the sin of the world" (John 1:29). His was the true sacrifice for sin that was foreshadowed in the law of Moses. (This sacrifice is also alluded to in the second chapter of the Qur'an, which is precisely entitled "the Heifer" or "the Cow" [verses 67–71; compare Num 19:1–10].)

God raised Jesus Christ from the dead and lifted him up to himself. His resurrection and ascension are evidence that he has perfectly accomplished his mission. He is a well-qualified mediator as well as an effective intercessor. Since he ascended to heaven, he has been interceding on our behalf:

> If God is for us, who can be against us? He who did not spare his own Son, but gave him up for us all—how will he not also, along with him, graciously give us all things? Who will bring any charge against those whom God has chosen? It is God who justifies. Who is then is the one who condemns? No one. Christ

71

Jesus who died—more than that, who was raised to life—is at the right hand of God and is also interceding for us. (Rom 8:31–34; confer Heb 7:23–28)

ISLAMIC OBJECTIONS TO THE CRUCIFIXION OF CHRIST

The death and resurrection of Jesus Christ are the foundational events for God's forgiveness: "God was reconciling the world to himself in Christ" (2 Cor 5:19). Muslims, however, believe that Jesus neither died nor was crucified. This belief is founded on the following Qur'anic passage:

> As for their [i.e., the Jews] claim that they killed the Messiah Jesus, son of Mary, the messenger of God, the truth is they did not kill him nor did they crucify him. They were under the illusion that they had. ... Assuredly, they did not kill him. On the contrary, God raised him to Himself, and God is powerful and wise. (4:157–158)

According to Islamic tradition, when Jesus was about to be arrested, God stepped in to rescue his prophet. He vindicated Jesus and took him up to himself alive. God made another man look like Jesus. Neither the Roman soldiers nor the Jews realized that the man they had crucified was not Jesus: "They were under the illusion that they had crucified Jesus." Jesus will return to earth at the end of time. He will have a new mission, which, unlike the first one, will be greatly successful. He will fight against the antichrist and will defeat him. He will implement Islamic law and will rule the earth for a time. Jews will then believe in him as God's prophet, and Christians will be convinced that he is not the Son of God. Both Jews and Christians will then realize he was not crucified. He will lead a normal life before he dies. Muslims will bury him next to Muhammad in Medina. His death will give the signal for the general resurrection and the last judgment (43:61).[29]

The Qur'an gives no reason that God rescued Jesus while allowing many other prophets to be killed by the Jews (2:61, 91; 3:21, 112, 181; 4:155; 5:73). Muslim theologians have objected to the crucifixion of Jesus Christ on the grounds that it undermines God's attributes:

1. God's *faithfulness* to his prophet would be undermined if he let him down.

2. God's *power* would be challenged if his enemies succeeded in putting Jesus to death.

3. God's *sovereignty* is such that he does not need a sacrifice to forgive sin (4:48), hence Jesus' death was unnecessary.

4. God's *justice* rules out the atoning death of Jesus on two accounts. First, it is unacceptable for someone to be punished for sins he did not commit. Second, God holds everyone accountable for their own deeds (6:164; 99:7–8).

A CHRISTIAN RESPONSE

The historicity of Jesus' crucifixion is based on the four Gospels, whose reliability cannot be seriously called into question (as seen in chapter 2). Christians believe that the crucifixion and resurrection of Christ perfectly fulfill all of God's attributes. God's righteousness was demonstrated in vindicating Jesus by raising him from the dead. His supreme power over evil is demonstrated in saving humanity from eternal death. God's sovereignty is best seen in his decision to save humankind through the incarnation, death, and resurrection of his Son. Just as God's love is limitless, so is his justice. God's love does not compromise with sin in any way, and his justice is absolute: "He does not leave the guilty unpunished" (Exod 34:7). He does not tolerate sin, not even the so-called minor sins. He wants to forgive our sins but not at the expense of his justice. The death of Jesus on our behalf displayed God's judgment on our sin. Jesus voluntarily offered his life for us. He thus demonstrated God's self-giving love for us in all its fullness (John 15:13). However, just because God saved humanity through Jesus' death and resurrection does not mean that everyone is saved. Our responsibility is fully engaged in the way we respond to God's forgiving love. Do we accept God's offer and live our lives accordingly, or do we dismiss it? Jesus summed up the gospel in two elements when he commissioned his disciples to be his witnesses in the world: forgiveness of sins and repentance (Luke 24:45–48). Forgiveness of sins is granted on the ground of what God has already done in Jesus Christ. It is unmerited; it is entirely founded not on our good deeds but on God's undeserved mercy toward us. It is one of God's greatest gifts to us. This saving grace is given freely to those who believe in him, but it cost Christ his own life. It is a powerful expression of God's unfailing love for his human creatures. Repentance signals our response to this grace. Do we acknowledge our sins, confess them to God, ask his forgiveness and commit ourselves to a new life? In other words, do we follow Jesus Christ as our Lord and Savior?

6

MUHAMMAD

Muslims claim that they believe in all God's prophets and discriminate against none. Jesus is one of their greatest prophets. They honor him and sometimes give his Qur'anic name, 'Isa, to their children. So why do Christians not do the same with Muslims? Why do they not reciprocate their inclusive faith? Why do they not believe in Muhammad as God's final prophet? Are they not being biased against Islam and prejudiced against Muslims?

Here are some possible answers to these questions often asked by Muslims:

1. Muslims are consistent with their Scriptures, which make it mandatory for them to believe in Jesus. Christians are also consistent with their own Scriptures, which do not speak of Muhammad.

2. Jesus himself compares the prophets who came before him to God's servants while he describes himself as God's Son who revealed God to the full (Matt 21:33–45; Heb 1:1–4). Therefore, there is no need for a prophet to come after him.

3. Muslims believe in the Qur'anic Jesus, not in the Christ of the Gospels. They do not, for instance, believe in the crucified and risen Christ.

4. What exactly do we mean by "prophet"? If a prophet is someone who preaches that the Creator is the one and only God and that everyone should worship him, then Muhammad could be seen as a prophet. But if the message of a "prophet" must be in line with the biblical revelation already given, it is surely understandable that Christians are dubious about the status of a "prophet" whose followers find no place for a sin-bearing, crucified, and resurrected Messiah.

5. More broadly, why should Christians accept Muhammad as a prophet? What is the positive evidence adduced in support of this claim? Is it convincing?

This section looks into the Islamic credentials for Muhammad's prophethood. They will be examined from a biblical perspective, just as Muslims assess Christian doctrine from a Qur'anic perspective. There are four main Islamic proofs for Muhammad's prophethood.

PROOF 1: BIBLICAL PROPHECIES

The Qur'an claims that Muhammad was foretold in both the Torah and the Injil (7:157), that is, in what Christians would call the Old and New Testaments. This Qur'anic claim is made with no proof text from either Scripture. By contrast the Gospels reproduce many quotations from the Torah to make the case that Jesus is indeed the long-awaited Messiah. The Jewish prophets predicted his birth, message, miracles, death, and resurrection.

The Islamic Prophetic Tradition (which was written down later than the Qur'an) refers to a text in Isaiah which speaks about "the Servant of the Lord."[30] This text needs to be viewed in its wider context. The prophet Isaiah portrays this servant in four poems known as "the Servant Songs." While some features of the servant may bear some similarities with Muhammad, others are characteristics of Jesus' mission. The fourth song, in particular, is about the suffering servant who offers his life as an atoning sacrifice. He is raised from the dead, lifted up to heaven, and honored by God, who appoints him as the qualified intercessor on our behalf (Isa 53).

Contemporary Muslims point to other texts in the Bible that in their view speak about Muhammad. Two passages are often cited in this respect. The first is the prophecy concerning the new Moses (Deut 18:15). Before he died Moses announced to his people that God would send them a prophet "like him." Muslim apologists argue that Muhammad is this prophet. Moses and Muhammad have many similarities in terms of their natural birth and death, their political and religious leadership, their supremacy over their enemies, and the comprehensiveness of their respective laws. Moses, however, foreshadowed Jesus in many more important features. Moses was God's prophet who mediated God's Word; Jesus was both God's prophet and God's word. Moses liberated his people from Pharaoh's political oppression; Jesus brought his people a far greater liberation, namely, a spiritual liberation, setting them free from the bondage of sin and eternal death. Moses interceded temporarily for his people after they worshiped the golden calf; Jesus has been our intercessor since the day he ascended to heaven and will always intercede for us. Jesus and Moses were both Jewish prophets, whereas Muhammad was not. Thus not only did Moses point to Jesus, but "the second Moses" is a far greater prophet than the first.

The second text concerns the Paraclete. Before he ascended to heaven, Jesus announced to his disciples that he would send them the *paraklētos*, a Greek word that means advocate, helper, comforter, or counselor (John 16:7, 12–13). Muslim apologists argue that Muhammad is the object of this prophecy. This claim is based on a Qur'anic text where Jesus is said to have predicted the coming of "Ahmad" (another name for Muhammad) after him (61:6). Again, this text from the Qur'an offers no

Scriptural reference to back up its assertion. Moreover, Jesus describes the one who was to come after him as "the Holy Spirit" (John 14:26), "the Spirit of truth" (John 14:16–17; 15:26). Furthermore, he told his disciples to stay in Jerusalem where the Spirit would be sent to them "in a few days" (Acts 1:4–5). Ten days after he ascended to heaven, the Holy Spirit was indeed sent to the disciples while they were gathered in Jerusalem (Acts 2:1–4). Thus these biblical texts point to a spiritual entity (the Holy Spirit), not to a physical, human entity (Muhammad).

PROOF 2: MIRACLES

A second Islamic proof that Muhammad was God's prophet is that he worked miracles. Jews, Christians, and Muslims all believe that some miracles are given by God to accredit his messengers. The Islamic Prophetic Tradition reports several miracles attributed to Muhammad.[31] Muhammad's greatest miracle, however, according to Islamic teaching, was the Qur'an itself (17:88; 52:34). This miracle points to the perfection of the Qur'an in terms of both its content and literary form. It is enhanced by the belief that Muhammad was illiterate (7:157–58) and thus unprepared to produce such an outstanding book. (The Qur'anic message will be considered under the third proof.)

The belief about Muhammad's illiteracy rests primarily on one text that describes him as an *ummi* prophet (7:157–58). To understand this word, one must examine its four other occurrences in Qur'anic texts. (1) Some Jews are blamed for being "illiterate," that is, ignorant of the Torah (2:78). (2) Muhammad was sent to "the People of the Book" as well as to "the illiterates," that is, peoples with no Holy Scripture (3:20). (3) Some people (Jews) among "the People of the Book" declare that they have no obligation toward "the illiterates," namely, the Arab people (3:75). (4) The "illiterates" (Arabs) were sent a prophet, namely Muhammad, from among themselves (62:2). These four texts show that the word *ummi* in the Qur'anic context is about religious ignorance, not about being unable to read and write. To take sura 7 verses 157–58 to mean that Muhammad was literally an illiterate prophet is an unwarranted interpretation. It aims to underscore the so-called miracle of the Qur'an. The likely meaning of the word is that as an Arab prophet Muhammad was not versed in the "Holy Scripture" (whether the reference is to the Bible or to the Qur'an) until the Qur'an was revealed to him.

The so-called supernatural literary style of the Qur'an can be appreciated only by Arabic speakers. The literary quality of any book is relative and subjective as it depends on our personal judgment. As for the Qur'an itself, not all Arabic-speaking people (including Muslims) agree that it is a masterpiece in Arabic literature. Furthermore, even if we accept the miraculous character of the Qur'an, miracles represent only one indicator that needs to be corroborated by other indicators. A self-proclaimed prophet should be judged by the content of his message regardless of whether he is able to work miracles (Deut 13:1–3). False prophets do sometimes work miracles (Matt 7:21–23; 24:24), and not all prophets have worked miracles. John the Baptist was a genuine prophet though he worked no miracles at all (John 10:41).

PROOF 3: ISLAMIC LAW

Muslim scholars argue that, unlike Jewish and Christian teaching, Islamic doctrine is perfect, which proves its divine origin. They make their case by looking at different aspects of this law.

According to Muslim apologists, religious law in Islam has the right balance between justice, which characterizes Judaism, and mercy, which is exemplified in Christianity. Islam is neither a violent religion (Judaism) nor an unrealistically pacifist religion (Christianity). Muslims see Judaism as focused on this world and Christianity as an other-worldly religion. Islam, by contrast, claims to contain the balance by focusing as much on life in this world as in the next.

Love and justice go hand in hand in Christianity, too. Christians have been mandated to preach the gospel, which is essentially about God's forgiving love, whereas civil authorities have been mandated by God to implement justice in society (Rom 13:1–4). Christians are not all pacifists: many, perhaps most, adhere to "just war" theory. Like Islam, biblical Christianity is a holistic religion that does not separate spiritual life from social, economic, and political life. Christians, however, do not take the same approach as Muslims as to how they should carry out their mission. Their emphasis is on individuals as much as on the community, on the need to change people's hearts as well as their behavior, and this change has to be bottom-up rather than top-down.

The Islamic penal code is seen by Muslims to be perfectly balanced. The death penalty is prescribed in only three cases (apostasy, murder, and adultery). Mosaic law is seen to be too harsh because capital punishment is prescribed in too many cases, whereas Christianity simply does not have a codified criminal system.

Yet this understanding of Christianity should be disputed. The fact that Christians are expected to forgive those who do them wrong (Matt 18:21–22) does not invalidate the state's obligation to fulfill its God-given mandate (Matt 22:21; Rom 13). Governments are established to elaborate and operate a just legal, political, and economic system that should remain adjustable according to times, places, and cultures.

Moral teaching is also deemed well balanced in the Qur'an, unlike the Torah and the New Testament. The Torah is seen to be too lax (for instance, unlimited polygamy, easy divorce) and the New Testament too strict (no divorce, no polygamy). By contrast, Islamic law combines human weakness and high moral standards (polygamy is limited to four wives, divorce is legal but reprehensible).

Yet Christian teaching does recognize human weakness. For instance, divorce is not completely ruled out

(Matt 5:31–32). At the same time, Christians are called to be perfect and merciful like their heavenly Father (Matt 5:48; Luke 6:36). The right ethical standards for God's people can only be God's moral perfection. One of God's most wonderful gifts is his Holy Spirit, who empowers believers in such a way that it is possible for them to model their lives on God's perfection embodied in the life of Jesus Christ. And one day, in the resurrection life of the new heaven and the new earth, that perfection will be perfectly achieved. Even now, while we live in anticipation of what is not yet but what will be, it is crucially important simultaneously to hold high the standard of perfection toward which we press, even while we lament our countless lapses—and then turn to the cross, once again, for forgiveness.

PROOF 4: MILITARY AND POLITICAL SUCCESS

Muslim scholars consider that Muhammad's triumph over his enemies is proof that he was God's prophet. When he died in AD 632, virtually all Arabs had embraced Islam. This is seen as evidence that Islam is a God-given religion, spread through the Prophet Muhammad. Today the Muslim community and the Christian community are about the same size (although the majority of human beings are neither Christian nor Muslim).

By contrast, Christianity does not equate religious, military, or political success with faithfulness to God. According to both the Bible (Heb 11:37–40) and the Qur'an (2:61, 91), many of God's faithful servants and prophets have been martyred. Jesus himself was very suspicious of popular success and worldly power (Matt 4:8–10; John 6:15). The question is, "What is genuine success?" The crucifixion of Jesus was a spectacular failure if we look at it from a human perspective. From God's perspective it was his greatest success because on the cross he defeated humanity's real enemies, namely, sin, evil, and death (Col 2:13–15). God demonstrated Jesus' victory when he raised him from the dead and enthroned him in heaven (Phil 2:9–11).

In short, from a Christian perspective, the four main proofs of Muhammad's prophethood are not conclusive. Christians are more than happy to own the first part of the Islamic creed: "There is no god but God." But it is not possible for them to make theirs the second part: "and Muhammad is his Apostle." To be sure, Muhammad was certainly a great religious and social reformer and an outstanding political and military leader. But the Christian creed highlights both God's oneness and Jesus' uniqueness: "There is one God and one mediator between God and mankind, the man Christ Jesus, who gave himself as a ransom for all people" (1 Tim 2:5–6).

7

THE KINGDOM OF GOD

B OTH THE BIBLE and the Qur'an stress the universal sovereignty of God. The Bible describes God as "the God of heaven and earth" (Gen 24:3; Matt 11:25); the Qur'an describes God as "the King of heaven and earth" (2:107; 3:189). Both Islam and Christianity teach that the kingdom of God has been established on earth. The coming of Jesus Christ for Christians and the revelation of the Qur'an for Muslims have ushered human history into a new phase. In the two religions, the revelation of the gospel (Acts 17:30) and the birth of Islam (3:154; 5:50; 33:33; 48:26), respectively, have brought the era of ignorance to an end. A new era has begun with the coming of God's kingdom among all the peoples of the world, especially among the community of believers.

Christianity and Islam are both missionary religions. Christians have been mandated to be God's witnesses on earth and to expand his kingdom (Luke 24:45–48). Muslims have received a similar mandate (2:143; 22:78; 33:45). How Christians and Muslims are to carry out their mission is dictated by the respective messages of Jesus Christ and Muhammad and the way they have preached the gospel and the Qur'an.

TWO MOVEMENTS IN
OPPOSITE DIRECTIONS

When we look into the Bible and the Qur'an, we are bound to notice a clear opposition as regards the development of their teachings about the expansion of God's kingdom. Put in simple terms, holy war in the Old Testament becomes spiritual warfare in the New Testament, whereas spiritual warfare in Mecca is subsumed under holy war in Medina.

JESUS

Until the time of Jesus, the Israelites lived under the covenant God made with the people of Israel through Moses. The Israelites were then under a theocratic government. All aspects of their lives were regulated by God's law, which was comprehensive in scope (religious, social, moral, economic, political, etc.). Because of sin and the resulting danger of human beings wielding too much power, God did not want the three offices under the old covenant (king, prophet, and priest) to be united in one person. In other words, even though the regime was theocratic, authority was divided: Israel was required to respect a distinction among these offices (and a strict separation between king and priest) so as to minimize the danger of authoritarianism.

Through military conquest, or holy war, under the leadership of Moses and his successor Joshua, the Israelites took possession of the land God had promised their ancestors. The nation of Israel had its hour of glory during the reign of David, who was a prophet before he became a king and a military chief. His name is associated not only with the many psalms he composed but with the conquest of the city of Jerusalem, which he made the capital of his kingdom (1 Chron 11:4–9). The military career of David by no means reflected God's perfect character. Because of the succession of wars that marked his reign, God refused to let David carry out his plan to build him a house, that is, a temple (1 Chron 28:3). God did not want the holiness of his house to be compromised by the violence that had sullied David's life.

The coming of Jesus introduced a radical change in the way God's kingdom is to be extended. The gospel is sometimes called "the gospel of the kingdom" (Matt 4:23; 9:35; 24:14). Jesus points to the imminent coming of God's kingdom, which is closely associated with faith in the gospel, the good news: "After John was put in prison, Jesus went into Galilee, proclaiming the good news of God. 'The time has come,' he said. 'The kingdom of God has come near. Repent and believe the good news!' " (Mark 1:14–15). The good news, the gospel, is all about the dawning of God's saving kingdom among all people. It brings sinners into reconciliation with God; it brings healing, deliverance, justice, forgiveness, and reconciliation among human beings (Luke 4:16–27).

By his presence, teaching, actions, death, and resurrection, Jesus not only revealed God's kingdom but put it into operation (Matt 12:28). He insisted this kingdom would not be established with visible power and splendor

(Luke 17:20–21; see especially the parables of the kingdom, Matt 13). It is in no way spectacular, at least as long as the "end" has not taken place (Matt 10:22; 24:6, 13–14). Jesus spoke of an end to history, an end inaugurated by his coming. At that point he comes to establish God's kingdom "with power" (Mark 9:1). Moreover he calls this kingdom his kingdom (Matt 16:28).

God's kingdom, embodied in Jesus' mission, has three main characteristics:

1. It is a *spiritual kingdom*, different from and above the political powers of this world. Jesus said that his kingdom was not of this world but of a heavenly one (John 18:36). On one occasion he had to slip away from the crowd when they were about to carry him off and make him king by force (John 6:15). The Jewish people, including some of Jesus' own disciples, were very disappointed that he did not have on his agenda the liberation of Israel from Roman occupation (Luke 24:19–27; Acts 1:6–8). Jesus claimed political leadership neither for himself nor for his disciples. He did not want his authority to be identified with any particular political system or power: "Give back to Caesar what is Caesar's, and to God what is God's" (Matt 22:21).

2. It is a *non-violent kingdom*. Jesus never used force, let alone violence, to overcome his enemies or to bring people into the kingdom. He wanted to convince people with the power of God's word, not with the sword. When he was arrested, he put up no resistance. To the great dismay of his disciples, he preferred to allow himself to be killed rather than resort to violence, even in self-defense (John 18:10–11). He pointed out the vicious circle of violence: "All who draw the sword will die by the sword" (Matt 26:52). Nailed to a cross bearing the inscription "This is Jesus, the king of the Jews," all that Jesus' enemies heard from his lips was "Father, forgive them, for they do not know what they are doing" (Luke 23:34). Thus, living in God's kingdom means loving one's enemies, and this precludes all forms of holy war, and still more personal vengeance: "You have heard that it was said, 'Love your neighbor and hate your enemy.' But I tell you, love your enemies and pray for those who persecute you, that you may be children of your Father in heaven" (Matt 5:43–45; confer Rom 12:14).

3. It is a *universal kingdom* whose interests transcend national interests. Jesus refers to the time

separating his first coming from his advent in glory and the full establishment of the kingdom of God as "the time of the Gentiles [or the nations]" (Luke 21:24). This time is the period allocated to all the nations of the earth to have access to salvation through the gospel (Rom 11:25–26). Jesus' mission has indeed made God's kingdom accessible to all nations (Acts 1:8).

The gospel is the main vehicle of extending God's kingdom on earth. It focuses on God's unchanging and redeeming love for humanity. The message of Jesus Christ, his life and his death and resurrection, encapsulate this love. The death and resurrection of Jesus Christ from the dead constitute the cornerstone of the Christian faith. Through his victory over sin and death, Jesus ushered humanity into a new and eternal life, a great and everlasting hope. The gospel calls people to acknowledge Jesus Christ as their Lord and Savior. A day is coming when everyone who has not believed in him as their king will have to submit to him as their Judge (Matt 25:31–46; Acts 17:30–31; Phil 2:9–11).

MUHAMMAD

The Qur'an presents the Prophet Muhammad as a model for all believers (33:21), and the Hadith provides information about his life and teaching. The Qur'anic message centers on "Islam," which means surrender, capitulation, and submission to God the Creator. Submission to God requires obedience to his law (shari'a). The word "islam" comes from the same root as "salam" (peace). Submitting to God brings peace between God and people. Historically it meant peace between Muslims and their polytheistic opponents (5:33–34).

For twelve years (AD 610–22), the Prophet preached Islam to his unbelieving fellow citizens, the people of Mecca. This message provoked much hostility; only a few dozen responded positively. God told Muhammad to be patient (43:88–89) and lenient with his enemies: "The Hour is surely coming; therefore forgive them with gracious forgiveness" (15:85). The preaching of Muhammad was to be done peacefully: "Call men to the path of your Lord with wisdom and kindly exhortation; argue with them in the best possible way" (16:125). Muslims were also invited to deal with "the People of the Book" (that is, Jews and Christians) "in the best possible way" (29:46; confer 3:64).

In 622, Muhammad made a critical decision that had far-reaching repercussions on his ministry. Faced with the opposition of his people in Mecca, he migrated with his companions to Medina. The number of Muslims grew rapidly. At the same time, conflict arose with the Jews of Medina. Together with the polytheistic Arabs of Mecca they were accused of conspiring against Muhammad. In this context the Prophet took on new responsibilities and became a political leader and an army commander. The content of the Qur'anic revelation also evolved. The "verse about the sword" was revealed, enjoining the Muslim community to fight against their enemies (9:5). "Holy War" was thus not only permitted but was made mandatory upon Muhammad and his followers according to a very well-known prophetic saying:

> I have been commanded to wage war against men as long as they do not say, "There is no god but God." As soon as they make this confession, I have no rights over their lives and possessions—unless they commit an offence against God's law. They are accountable only to God.[32]

In 624, the struggle against the Jews of Medina reached a turning point, and they were all eradicated. In 630, the Muslim army triumphantly entered Mecca, having obtained the surrender of its leaders. This victory was immediately followed by the establishment of monotheistic worship in the temple of the Ka'aba. Many Arab tribes embraced the new religion, not always out of conviction (49:13). In the next few years, the number of Muslims increased greatly, gaining an ever-stronger influence throughout the region. Muslims were still committed to preaching Islam, but the preaching was now reinforced by force if necessary. "The People of the Book" were not forced to convert to Islam, but they had to submit to Islamic rule and pay a poll-tax (9:29). In 632, Muhammad died, having been hailed by the majority of Arabs not only as a Prophet, but also as a great social reformer, an exceptionally charismatic politician, and a talented military leader.

God's kingdom in Islam is a universal rule; the Prophet was sent to all peoples (3:20; 21:107). It is a rule of this world as much as of the next. The Muslim community is to obey God's law as revealed during the second period of the Prophet's mission in Medina. This means that Muslims are under obligation to resort to force if they come under attack or if they are prevented from preaching Islam. Jihad (literally "struggle") is about a resolute and total commitment to the cause of God. In the event of God's cause and the Muslim community being endangered, Muslims must take up arms and fight their enemies, even if they are reluctant to do battle (2:216; 4:77). Armed combat or holy war is therefore a legitimate form of jihad. A saying attributed to the Prophet has it that "the *mujahid* [fighter] is he who enters the fight against his own soul."[33] Thus jihad as spiritual warfare complements without contradicting or invalidating jihad as military expedition.

Islamic law ensures that God's rule is being implemented in the Muslim community. Like Jewish law, shari'a is all-embracing, regulating all aspects of human life (religious, social, economic, etc.) for both individuals and the community. The law of retaliation given in the Torah (Lev 24:17–21) is in force in the shari'a too (5:45). Islamic penal code requires the death penalty in three cases: murder, apostasy, and sexual immorality.[34] It also prescribes physical punishments for certain offences: hand mutilation for theft (5:38) and flogging for wrongly accusing a married Muslim woman of adultery (24:4–5) and for consuming alcohol.[35]

HOLY WAR AND THE GOSPEL

Walking in the steps of their master, the disciples of Jesus took the gospel to the Jewish people and far beyond. Within one generation the gospel reached most Mediterranean countries and cities, including Rome, the capital of the Roman empire. Christians never used force to support their preaching. For three centuries Christians lived as a religious minority and were sometimes persecuted. Following the conversion of Emperor Constantine, Christianity became the religion of the Empire. Christianity became the state religion, and in this context some Christian theologians developed the concept of "just war," a concept that demands that several strict criteria be met before a war can be justified. Even in this context these theologians avoided using the expression "holy war," and in general they saw "just war" to be the responsibility of government, not the church.

The collusion of Christianity and government in Christendom has sometimes led to religious persecution (against fellow Christians, Jews, and "heretical" Christians) and to religious wars against non-Christians (the Crusades, for example). This religious violence dishonored Christ's name. Christians today are ashamed of all sorts of violence done by their fellow Christians in different parts of the world throughout history (anti-Semitism, Crusades, apartheid, ethnic cleansing, xenophobia). In many countries in the world, including Western countries, the Christian community represents a religious minority, as was the case during the first centuries. This brings us back to the teaching of Jesus Christ and his disciples. The only holy war that is legitimate from a Christian perspective is spiritual warfare (Eph 6:10–17). In the Lord's Prayer, Christians ask for God's kingdom to come on earth as in heaven (Matt 6:9–13). This amounts to pleading with God that many people will accept Jesus Christ as their heavenly King and that the kingdom values (God-centeredness, reconciliation to God, justice, peace, love, forgiveness, and truth) will grow in our world.

JIHAD AND SHARI'A

The historic role of the Prophet in Islam exemplifies the global character of Islamic law. He was at the same time prophet, political leader, social reformer, and military commander. Likewise, Islam has traditionally been understood as religion and government and as a religion for life in this world and in the next.

By the time the Prophet died, all Arabia had come under Islamic rule. The first four caliphs, known as the rightly guided caliphs, took upon themselves the responsibility of spreading Islam as far as possible. To a large degree, they succeeded. Damascus fell to Muslims in 635, Jerusalem in 638, Egypt and Persia in 642, soon followed by North Africa, Spain in the West, and the Indian subcontinent in the East. In 732, exactly one hundred years after the Prophet's death, the Muslim army experienced its first major defeat near Poitiers (center of France). By then Islam had taken control of vast territories, including territories traditionally regarded as Christian. Muslim scholars have seen in the rapid and spectacular Islamic conquests, a clear sign of Islam's divine origin.

Gradually but surely, Islamic law was implemented in the newly conquered territories. Christians (and Jews) found themselves living as second-class citizens in the Islamic Empire because of their protected minority status.[36] This status was meant to protect their lives and possessions as a religious minority, but it did not give them equality with Muslim citizens. In fact they often came under pressure and sometimes under open persecution. Many eventually converted to Islam. Shari'a law still represents the main source of legislation in numerous Islamic countries. This means that Christian communities still face serious forms of discrimination in these countries.[37]

THE BATTLE BETWEEN ISLAMIC REFORM AND ISLAMIC RADICALISM

With up to 25 percent of the Muslim population worldwide living in non-Islamic countries today, many Muslims have been led to look afresh at shari'a teaching. Reformers have come to the conclusion that Islamic law, including its penal code, needs to be revisited and possibly updated to fit modern societies. They are aware that Islam has often been used and abused by Muslim politicians and religious leaders to reinforce their own positions. They point out that the Qur'an commands Muslims to conduct their affairs by "mutual consultation" (42:38), in the same way the Prophet dealt with his community (3:159). They see in these texts and others the seeds for Islamic reform and democracy. In Mecca, they observe, Muhammad was primarily a prophet. In Medina he took on political leadership coincidentally because he happened to be the best man for the job at the time. In other words, Islam does not have to be closely associated with political power and public life.

Reformist Muslims also highlight that the Qur'an promotes religious freedom: "Let there be no coercion in religion" (2:256; confer 5:102; 10:99).[38] They understand jihad in terms of religious, social, and political struggle intended to implement necessary reforms and to address the ills of Muslim societies (illiteracy, corruption, unemployment, etc.). Their reading of Islamic sources (Qur'an and Hadith) is contextual and rational.

Islamic radicalism has also witnessed a revival in recent years. Muslim radicals follow a literal understanding of Islamic foundational texts. They want to see shari'a fully implemented in Muslim societies. Their popularity seems to increase when the Muslim community experiences some form of injustice (economic exploitation, social deprivation, political oppression). Muslim extremists go one step further. They use and often misuse Islamic Scriptures to justify terrorist acts against their fellow Muslims (seen as nominal, heretical, or hypocritical Muslims) and against Western countries (accused of supporting corrupt Islamic regimes). The battle to win the hearts and minds of Muslims is relentless between reformist and radical Muslims. How this will play out over time cannot be gauged with any degree of confidence. But certainly the history of the church in Europe and elsewhere should humble us and prevent us from being judgmental as we consider how Muslim societies are struggling with the role of religion in politics.

8

CONCLUDING
REFLECTIONS

TRANSPARENTLY, CHRISTIANS AND Muslims share some common commitments. Together with Jews, we share a deep commitment to monotheism—though admittedly Christians invoke a complex monotheism (trinitarianism) that Jews and Muslims alike disavow. The best of the three traditions hungers for a God-centeredness that stands over against endless self-seeking or mere consumerism. The first responsibility of sentient creatures is to recognize their creatureliness, and this, too, the three traditions share. Out of this matrix springs a nest of other common values (though they are often worked out in different ways): a high valuation of family, a commitment to fellow believers, and a concern for fellow human beings.

Yet Christians and Muslims will be less than candid with each other if they do not acknowledge their profound differences. While both believe that the kingdom of God has dawned and will one day be consummated, the time of that dawning and the nature of the kingdom are both contested. The one side sees the kingdom coming in the person, death, resurrection, and exaltation of Christ, working out now in the powerful transformation of individuals by the gospel of Christ, constituting a people, a church, that longs for the consummation of resurrection existence when Jesus returns; the other side sees the kingdom coming in the triumphant successes of Islam, including military ones, especially during its first century, with people learning to submit to God as he is disclosed through Muhammad, God's will made known in shari'a. The imitation of Christ leads to one sort of religion; the imitation of Muhammad, who was a mighty warrior as well as a powerful preacher, leads to another.

Above all, the means by which fallen human beings may be reconciled to God are fundamentally at odds in the two traditions. In biblically-faithful Christianity, the grace of God crowns everything, as guilty human beings are reconciled to their Maker by the sacrifice that God himself has provided in Jesus' death on the cross. Christians are empowered by the Holy Spirit to live repentant and obedient lives that they would not otherwise choose. In Islam, while appeal is made to the mercy of God, the hope of paradise rests fundamentally on personal obedience to God, repentance, scrupulous avoidance of major sins, and confidence that one's good deeds will in some way atone for one's bad deeds.

At the heart of the polarization between Christianity and Islam lies the divergent historical assessments of Jesus and of Muhammad. The claims of the two religions cannot both be true: they are, as we have seen, intrinsically exclusive. Such recognition never warrants hate or malice: surely both sides are obligated to tell the truth as they understand it, yet such truth-telling should be undertaken with courtesy, respect, attentive listening. When the truth claims are mutually contradictory, and the issues of such transcendental importance, faithful witness equally demands honest and respectful confrontation, frank and courteous debate. The issues will be not only theological but historical. For instance, if it be established, so far as history can establish anything, that Jesus rose from the dead,[39] the implications are sweeping not only for understanding who Jesus is and for what he accomplished on the cross, but also for any system of thought that depends, in whole or in part, on the denial of this claim.

Acknowledgments

T HE SERIES Questions for Restless Minds is produced by the Christ on Campus Initiative, under the stewardship of the editorial board of D. A. Carson (senior editor), Douglas Sweeney, Graham Cole, Dana Harris, Thomas McCall, Geoffrey Fulkerson, and Scott Manetsch. The editorial board recognizes with gratitude the many outstanding evangelical authors who have contributed to this series, as well as the sponsorship of Trinity Evangelical Divinity School (Deerfield, Illinois), and the financial support of the MAC Foundation and the Carl F. H. Henry Center for Theological Understanding. The editors also wish to thank Christopher Gow, who created the study questions accompanying each book, and Todd Hains, our editor at Lexham Press. May God alone receive the glory for this endeavor!

Study Guide Questions

1. What is the difference between inspiration and recitation? What are some implications that come from the fact that the Christian Scriptures were inspired rather than recited?

2. How do you feel about naming God "Father" in what ways is it helpful/unhelpful?

3. How does Moucarry respond to the objection that Jesus never claimed he was God? How would you make the case that the Bible affirms Jesus' divinity?

4. How do the two religions differ in their understanding of sin? Forgiveness?

5. Muslims contend that God's character would not allow him to let Jesus be killed (73). What aspects of God's character are displayed in his letting Jesus be killed?

6. Moucarry says that Muslims say they believe in Jesus (79–80). How would you respond to a Muslim who said they believe in Jesus?

7. What are the major differences between the two depictions of the Kingdom of God?

8. What do you think are the most important points of agreement between Islam and Christianity? What about disagreement?

9. How could what you've learned enable to you to better love your Muslim neighbors this week?

For Further Reading

Brown, Daniel W. *A New Introduction to Islam*. 2nd ed. Blackwell, 2007.

> Solid and well-balanced look at Islamic teaching and history. Considers alternative expressions of faith in the Muslim community (e.g., mystical Islam, political Islam).

Chapman, Colin. *Cross and Crescent: Responding to the Challenges of Islam*. IVP, 2007.

> A sympathetic and critical approach to Islamic teaching and practice. Examines a whole range of issues relevant to Christian-Muslim relationships from an evangelical Christian perspective. Excellent introduction to Christian-Muslim issues.

Cragg, Kenneth. *The Call of the Minaret*. 3rd ed. Oneworld, 2000.

> First published in 1956 and regularly reprinted, this is Cragg's first major work. He is a leading Christian

scholar of Islam and a prolific writer. His interaction with Islam is profound, appreciative, and mission-minded.

Deedat, Ahmed. *The Choice: Islam and Christianity*. 2 vols. Adam, 2007.

A collection of booklets written by the most popular Muslim propagandist worldwide who has debated several Christian leaders. Overtly polemical and typical of a confrontational Muslim approach to Christianity.

Kurzman, Charles, ed. *Liberal Islam: A Source Book*. Oxford University Press, 1998.

This is a compilation of very significant articles written by reformist Muslim scholars. They examine a number of key sensitive issues (e.g., women in Islam, Islamic criminal code, human rights, the relation between the state and religion). They all advocate a fresh and critical look at Islamic Scriptures and tradition.

Moucarry, Chawkat. *The Prophet and the Messiah: An Arab Christian's Perspective on Islam and Christianity*. IVP, 2001.

Moucarry engages apologetically with Islamic doctrine as Muslim theologians themselves understand it. In addition, *The Prophet and the Messiah*, and the British edition entitled *Faith to Faith: Christianity and Islam in Dialogue,* expand on the themes discussed in this book.

Ramadan, Tariq. *Islam, the West and the Challenges of Modernity.* Islamic Foundation, 2003.

One of the most influential Muslim leaders in Europe, Ramadan believes Islam has a distinctive contribution to make to Western societies. The role of Muslims is to be God's witnesses, bold and creative, in an increasingly secular civilization.

Notes

1. Unless otherwise specified, numbers of this sort, appealing to the authority of Islam, are to the Qur'an.
2. Eckhard Schnabel, *Early Christian Mission* (IVP, 2004), 2:1585–86.
3. The Hebrew and the Greek words for "testament" can also mean "covenant." The Old Testament refers to the covenant God made with the people of Israel through Moses, and the New Testament to the covenant God made with humanity through Jesus Christ. The Qur'an uses the words "Torah" and "Injil" for the two parts of the Bible. This book sometimes adopts terminology analogous to this Qur'an usage: that is, the word "gospel" may stand for the message of Jesus Christ (the "Injil") that is found in the four Gospels and in the other writings of the New Testament. At other times this book uses the traditional Christian nomenclature of "Old Testament" and "New Testament."

4. The "People of the Book" have a special status in Islam. Unlike polytheistic people, they have the right to live alongside the Muslim community as protected minorities. They do not have to convert to Islam but they must submit to Islamic rule (9:29).

5. The two figures in brackets refer to the year the named scholar died, the first according to the Islamic calendar and the second to the Christian calendar.

6. Some Muslims today contend that the Bible, unlike the Qur'an, contradicts science, which proves its corruption. This view is found in M. Bucaille, *The Bible, the Qur'an and Science: The Holy Scriptures Examined in the Light of Modern Knowledge* (American Trust Publications, 1979). A Christian response to this book is available in W. Campbell, *The Qur'an and the Bible in the Light of History and Science* (Middle-East Resources). Classical Muslim theologians never use this science-based argument. Another argument used by contemporary Muslim apologists is that the so-called Gospel of Barnabas is the authentic Gospel given by God to Jesus. This pseudo-gospel, written probably in the thirteenth century by an Italian convert to Islam, contradicts the Qur'an on many points (e.g., Muhammad, not Jesus, is described as the Messiah).

7. See Carl F. H. Henry, "Bible, Inspiration of," *Evangelical Dictionary of Theology*, ed. Walter A. Elwell, 2nd ed. (Baker, 2001), 159–63. See also the two volumes edited by D. A. Carson and John D. Woodbridge: *Scripture and Truth* (Zondervan, 1983) and *Hermeneutics, Authority, and Canon* (Zondervan, 1986).

8. I. Faruqi et al., *Christian Mission and Islamic Da'wah* (Islamic Foundation, 1982), 48.

9. See Craig L. Blomberg, "Jesus of Nazareth: How Historians Can Know Him and Why It Matters," Christ on Campus Initiative, 2008, http://www.thegospelcoalition.org/pdf/blomberg.pdf.

10. Most Arab linguists consider "Allah" to be the contraction of the definite article *al* and the Arabic word for God, *ilah*, such that the literal meaning of *Allah* is "the God." The word *ilah* derives from a root carrying the ideas of adoration, protection, eternity, power, and creation. Others think *Allah* is God's proper name, which has no derivation. The Arabic word for God is similar to what we have in other Semitic languages: Aramaic (*Elah*), Syriac (*Alaha*), and Hebrew (*El, Eloah, Elohim*).

11. The Hadith, or Prophetic Tradition, represents the record of the Prophet's life and teaching. There are nine "canonical compilations." The two lists of God's names are found in Tirmidhi (*da'awat* [invocations], 87) and Ibn Majah (*du'a'* [invocation], 10).

Twenty-six names are exclusive to each list. They are all reproduced in C. Moucarry, *Two Prayers for Today: The Lord's Prayer and the Fatiḥa* (Christava Sahittya Samithi, 2007), 125–30.

12. This saying is reported in various versions. See Bukhari, *istiʼdhan* [asking permission], 1; Muslim, *birr* [righteousness], 32.

13. In his tractate *The Ninety-Nine Beautiful Names of God,* trans. D. Burrell and N. Dahar (Islamic Texts Society, 1995), Abu Ḥamid al-Ghazali, a great Muslim theologian and mystic, explains the meaning of these names and how they apply to some degree to human beings.

14. John R. W. Stott, *Through the Bible through the Year* (Baker, 2006), 18.

15. John R. W. Stott, *The Message of the Sermon on the Mount* (IVP, 1978), 146. See also the important study of Jonathan T. Pennington, *Heaven and Earth in the Gospel of Matthew* (NovTSup 126; Brill, 2007).

16. Church leaders ascribed the title *theotokos* ("Mother of God") to the Virgin Mary at the Council of Chalcedon in 451. Nestorian Christians did not accept it.

17. As quoted in A. Hamman, *Le Notre Père dans l'Église ancienne. Choix de textes des Pères de l'Église* (Les Éditions Franciscaines, 1995), 134.

18. Gregory of Nyssa, quoted in Hamman, *Le Notre Père,* 77.

19. On Jesus' pre-existence, see now Simon J. Gathercole, *The Preexistent Son: Recovering the Christologies of Matthew, Mark, and Luke* (Eerdmans, 2006).

20. See C. Moucarry, *The Prophet and the Messiah: An Arab Christian's Perspective on Islam and Christianity* (IVP, 2001), 175–83.

21. The Qur'anic portrait of Jesus has many features that are found, not in the Gospels in the Bible (all written during the first century) but in the apocryphal gospels written in the second and third centuries. For example, the miracle of creating birds from clay is recorded not in the canonical gospels but in the opening short story of the Infancy Gospel of Thomas (2.1–5 [end of the second century]). Compare also the still later Arabic Infancy Gospel, with which Muhammad was apparently familiar.

22. Bukhari, *anbiya'* [prophets], 45.

23. Abu Ḥamid al-Ghazali follows this line of argument in his famous treatise *Al-Radd al-jamil li-ilahiyyat 'Isa bi-ṣariḥi l-injil*, ed. and trans. R. Chidiac as *Réfutation excellente de la divinité de Jésus-Christ d'après les évangiles*, Arabic-French ed. (Presses Universitaires de France, 1939).

24. This section represents a very brief summary of my book *The Search for Forgiveness: Pardon and Punishment in Islam and Christianity* (IVP, 2004).

25. Muslim, *iman* [faith], 37. This teaching is not entirely dissimilar to the Catholic doctrine about grave (or mortal) sins and venial sins.

26. Bukhari, *iman* [faith], 34.

27. Abu Dawud, *sunna* [behavior], 23.

28. Temporary punishment in hell in this theology is similar to Roman Catholicism's purgatory, and the Prophet's intercession is comparable to Roman Catholicism's "intercession of the saints."

29. Bukhari, *anbiya'* [prophets], 50; Muslim, *fitan* [seditions], 23.

30. Bukhari, *buyu'* [sales], 50; see Isaiah 42:1–9.

31. Bukhari, *manaqib* [virtues], 25.

32. Bukhari, *iman* [faith], 16.

33. Tirmidhi, *faḍa'il al-jihad* [virtues of jihad], 2.

34. Bukhari, *diyat* [blood money], 6. It is worth noting that the Mosaic law also prescribes capital punishment for murder (Deut 19:21), blasphemy (Lev 24:15–16), and adultery (Lev 20:10).

35. Bukhari, *ḥudud* [legal punishments], 3.

36. To be fair, for centuries the Jewish communities were badly treated in Europe. Christian anti-Semitism, however, had nothing to do with the teaching of Christ (who was himself a Jew).

37. Examples of such discrimination is that according to Islamic law a Muslim man can marry a Christian woman, but a Christian man cannot marry a Muslim woman (5:5); a Christian can convert to

Islam, but a Muslim will come under apostasy law if he converts to Christianity (Bukhari, *jihad*, 149). In some countries (e.g., Malaysia), if a Muslim becomes a Christian and is not executed for apostasy, he or she cannot marry a Christian because the legal status of the convert is still Muslim and the shari'a courts will not sanction the change. Christians may not take leadership roles in Muslim societies since Muslims must be governed by fellow Muslims.

38. Traditionally, this text has been understood in a restrictive sense: Jews and Christians should not be forced to convert to Islam, not that Muslims are free to convert to another religion.

39. One thinks, for instance, of the remarkable book by N. T. Wright, *The Resurrection of the Son of God* (Fortress, 2003).

LEXHAM PRESS

—

CLARIFYING ANSWERS ON QUESTIONS FOR RESTLESS MINDS

Series Editor: D. A. Carson

The Questions for Restless Minds series applies God's word to today's issues. Each short book faces tough questions honestly and clearly, so you can think wisely, act with conviction, and become more like Christ.

Learn more at lexhampress.com/questions